Pet Crafts

Pet Crafts

28 great toys, gifts and accessories for pet lovers

Heidi Boyd

NORTH LIGHT BOOKS
CINCINNATI, OHIO
www.artistsnetwork.com

Pet Crafts. Copyright © 2004 by Heidi Boyd. Printed in Singapore. All rights reserved. The patterns and drawings in the book are for the personal use of the reader. By permission of the author and publisher, they may be either hand-traced or photocopied to make single copies, but under no circumstances may they be resold or republished. It is permissible for the purchaser to make the projects contained herein and sell them at fairs, bazaars and craft shows. No other part of this book may be reproduced in any form or by any electronic or mechanical means, including information storage and retrieval systems, without permission in writing from the publisher, except by a reviewer, who may quote a brief passage in review. Published by North Light Books, an imprint of F&W Publications, Inc., 4700 East Galbraith Road, Cincinnati, Ohio 45236. (800) 289-0963. First edition.

Other fine North Light Books are available from your local bookstore or art supply store or direct from the publisher.

08 07 06 05 04   5 4 3 2 1
Library of Congress Cataloging-in-Publication Data
Boyd, Heidi.
Pet Crafts / by Heidi Boyd.
     p.cm.
Includes index.
ISBN 1-58180-503-9 (pbk. : alk. paper)
1. Handicraft. 2. Animals in art. 3. Pet supplies.
I. Title.

TT157.B725 2004
745.5--dc21

2003054133

EDITOR: Jolie Lamping Roth
COVER DESIGNER: Andrea Short
INTERIOR DESIGNER: Brian Roeth
ILLUSTRATIONS ON PAGES 13, 31, 47 & 67 BY: Heidi Boyd
PRODUCTION COORDINATOR: Sara Dumford
LAYOUT ARTIST: Kathy Gardner
PHOTOGRAPHERS: Christine Polomsky, Tim Grondin
     and Al Parrish
PHOTO STYLIST: Kimberly Brown

Metric Conversion Chart

TO CONVERT	TO	MULTIPLY BY
Inches	Centimeters	2.54
Centimeters	Inches	0.4
Feet	Centimeters	30.5
Centimeters	Feet	0.03
Yards	Meters	0.9
Meters	Yards	1.1
Sq. Inches	Sq. Centimeters	6.45
Sq. Centimeters	Sq. Inches	0.16
Sq. Feet	Sq. Meters	0.09
Sq. Meters	Sq. Feet	10.8
Sq. Yards	Sq. Meters	0.8
Sq. Meters	Sq. Yards	1.2
Pounds	Kilograms	0.45
Kilograms	Pounds	2.2
Ounces	Grams	28.4
Grams	Ounces	0.035

Artist Heidi Boyd creates innovative craft projects using a philosophy toward surprise and accessibility. In addition to *Pet Crafts*, Heidi authored the children's craft book *Fairy Crafts*, also by North Light Books. She's contributed proprietary projects to the kids' section of *Better Homes and Gardens*, *Crayola Kids* and *FamilyFun* magazines. Her work is featured in many of Meredith Corporation's craft publications, including *Crafts for Kids*, *Simply Handmade*, *Halloween Fun* and *501 Fun-to-Make Family Crafts*.

With a degree in fine arts, she has been an art instructor to children in schools and art centers for over a decade while pursuing her vocation as an illustration artist. She lives in Des Moines, Iowa, with her husband, Jon, sons, Jasper and Elliot, and dog, Maizy.

Dedicated to our family and neighborhood pets:

Maizy (soft-coated wheaten), Birdie (Chihuahua), Dagny (vizsla), Theo (black cat), Tim and Kitti-enn (tabby cats), Charlotte (Angora cat), Anna (collie mix), Lily and Casper (long-haired cats), Benny and Bingo (Italian greyhounds), Greta, Jasmine and Oscar (the cats who tolerate them), Maddie (Border collie and Australian shepherd mix), Mitzi and Bosco (miniature schnauzers), Tanner (vizsla) and Tramp (terrier mix), Jamie (Border collie), Abby (Airedale), Adam and Casey (huskies), Pete and Angus (shelties), Chooie and Tagus (Portuguese water dogs), Sheba and Inu (Shiba Inus) and Tan Cat (who is indeed a tan cat).

And also to Rajah (golden retriever mix), Modesty (tabby cat) and BlackJack (black short-haired cat) who are the inspiration behind Jolie Roth's pet-friendly editing.

Table of Contents

CHAPTER ONE

PET TOYS . . . 12

CHAPTER TWO

PET ACCESSORIES . . . 30

Introduction

Every day our crazy dog Maizy puts a smile on our faces. She watches after our two boys, joining in on all the fun and games. Whenever they walk out the door she follows at their heels not wanting to miss out on any adventures. During the school day she keeps me company in the studio, laying her soft head on my feet while I work. At the end of the day she's the first to greet my husband at the door, wrapping her front paws around his neck and covering his face with wet kisses.

This book is intended for families who share their homes and lives with a loving four-legged friend. It celebrates all breeds and animal personalities, from the playful cat who loves to pounce on fluttering feathers to the older dog that's content to spend his days sleeping on a fleece bed. Among the twenty-eight projects, you will find many that suit your cat or dog. For the playful pet the toy chapter is filled with balls to fetch, stuffed animals that squeak, mouse tails to paw and springy snakes to hunt. The pampered pet will appreciate the pet accessory chapter, which features matching collar and leash sets, personalized food bowls and place mats, and customized treat jars, all intended for daily use. The party animal will dig the celebration chapter, which has costumes and gifts for birthdays, Halloween and Christmas. There are also projects for people who love pets, photo albums for treasured photos, journals to record special memories and stuffed animals that can be crafted in your own pet's likeness.

My hope is that in the excitement of making a craft to celebrate your pet you'll learn a new skill. Every project has been broken into easy-to-follow steps that call for readily available materials. So get crafting and make a little something for your special pet. Once you see how easy it is, you'll want to make more for your neighbors', friends' and relatives' pets, too! It's a small repayment for the love and devotion animals reward us with every day.

9

Getting Started

The following is a list of some basic tools and materials needed to make the projects in this book. In addition, each project includes a detailed materials list. For the more specialized materials you may not have on hand, check out the Resource Guide on page 94 for easier shopping.

In this section, I've also provided some crafting tips for adults wanting to craft with their children. Many of the projects are ideal for beginners and will be fun for the whole family to make.

Sewing Machine

A sewing machine is a great piece of equipment to introduce to older children. After showing them how the machine works, sit with them and actively help them guide the fabric through the machine. The main concerns should be keeping fingers clear of the needle and presser foot area along with keeping the foot pedal engaged at an even controllable speed.

While hand stitching is an alternative, the Fleece Friends, Paw Wipe and Squeaky Squirrel are quicker and easier to machine stitch and the finished project will be more durable. For younger children the punched Christmas stockings and Squeaky Sock Snakes are both easy beginning sewing projects with simple hand stitching.

Glue Gun

Glue guns speed up the assembly process, creating an instant bond between materials. I strongly recommend using a smaller-size model with a low temperature setting. Keep a cup of ice nearby to provide instant relief in case of burns.

Beacon's Kids Choice Glue is a good alternative to a glue gun. It still provides a quick bond and when dry is more durable than hot glue.

Craft Knife

You'll need a craft knife while making the Cork Frame (see page 63) and Treat Gift Cards (see page 68). The blade is extremely sharp, and even older children should be supervised. Please follow all guidelines for knife safety: Work on a cutting board with a sharp blade, cut away from your body, work out of reach of other people, and carefully store the knife covered in a safe place.

Paint Markers and Glues

Paint markers and glues (such as Aleene's Platinum Bond and Beacon's Gem-Tac and Fabri-Tac) are specified for several projects so that the finished project will be durable and withstand contact with water. The primary concern while using paint markers, glues and any product that may give off fumes is ventilation, as inhaling the vapors could be harmful. These materials are not intended for young children's use, and should be used only in well-ventilated areas.

Safety

Simplicity and the reader's success were primary concerns while designing the crafts in this book. If you are crafting with children, certain equipment and procedures will require you to take an active role to protect them and ensure their success, and some equipment may not be suitable for younger children.

In addition, some projects in Chapter 3 For Kids Who Love Pets are more fitting for older children. Projects containing small parts and materials, such as the Fleece Friends on page 54, are not intended for children under three years of age.

Equipment Safety

For some projects an oven or iron is required. Please exercise caution while using the oven to cure the ceramic paint, polymer clay and shrink-art material used in the food bowls, treat canisters and vanity tags. Let the pieces cool completely before handling them.

The pet pillows call for the cat and dog appliqués to be ironed in place. Please exercise caution when using the iron. If your child would like to help with projects involving the oven or iron, have your child prepare the pieces for you to iron or bake as needed.

Pet Safety

The projects in this book have been designed for your pet's enjoyment and safety. Every effort has been made to use materials equivalent to those used in commercially manufactured items that are sold in pet stores. It is important to use all new materials and stuffing. Please take the time to find the appropriate glues, as anything that might be mouthed should be assembled with nontoxic glue. Please hand or machine stitch pieces together where specified to make a toy that will withstand active play.

Carefully supervise your pet while playing and quickly remove any loose parts. Keep broken toys out of reach until they're resewn or repaired. When selecting which projects to make for your pets take their size and play habits into consideration. For the most part the dog toys in this book are intended for light chewers. (I hope the larger dogs will accept my sincere apologies.)

You know what they say about all work and no play. This chapter is full of fun for dogs, cats and people, too! Playtime is a great way to bond with your pet, and can turn the shyest kitten or pup into a real showstopper.

PET TOYS

My neighbors' cat Casper, named for his timid ways, discovered an unexpected toy as a kitten. Their oldest child, Maggie, practiced the piano every day. Casper was intrigued by the piano, and doing what curious cats do, he hopped onto the bench beside her. Before long the rhythm must have gotten to him, because he reached out a paw and tapped an ivory key. Maggie and her mother were surprised to see the new kitten play the piano. They praised him and handed him treats. Casper figured out that pawing piano keys was generously rewarded and quickly became a piano-playing virtuoso. Casper has grown accustomed to being called upon to perform whenever company arrives. All treats are accepted.

But don't worry if your pet isn't musically inclined. This chapter has great toys your pet is sure to love.

Casper the Pianist

Kitten Mittens

When these pom-pom mice come on the scene, the cat is sure to come out to play. Pom-poms and fleece strips transform a regular work glove into a tantalizing cat toy. Slip a hand into the whimsical mitt and wiggle your fingers to jingle the bells and bring your cat out of hiding.

step one | Use scissors to trim one side of a small pompom into a cone-shaped mouse head.

step two | To assemble the mouse, hot glue one end of the 6" (15cm) fleece tail, large pom-pom body and shaped pom-pom head onto the center top of the glove.

step three | Finish the mouse by hot gluing the tiny pom-pom nose and eyes to the shaped pom-pom head.

Cut two rounded ears of felt, and then glue the flat ends of the ears between the back of the mouse head and body.

step four | Fold over one end of a fleece strip (approximately ⅛" [3mm]) and then hot glue the folded end to a glove fingertip. Repeat the process with the three remaining strips so that one hangs down from every glove fingertip except the thumb.

15

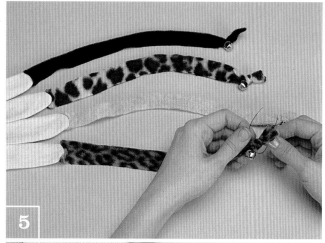

More Mice, Less Noise
Assemble a mouse on the end of each fingertip, so the fleece strips become tails (skip the bells). Write *Here Kitty Kitty* and then stamp paw prints around the lettering.

step five | Tie each fleece strip end in an overhand knot. Thread a 3" (8cm) length of elastic through the hole in a jingle bell and then tie and knot the elastic around a fleece strip just above the overhand knot. Trim the ends. Repeat the process to tie bells onto the remaining three strips.

step six | Using very light pressure, write *Squeek* in permanent marker on the top of the glove by the mouse.

Tug & Chew Rope

In a few minutes you can revamp knee-high stockings into a stretchy dog toy. The finished rope can be the center of play for a couple of dogs or the perfect chew toy for one.

MATERIALS: three knee-high stockings (or use three socks for more heft and less stretch) • cornstarch chew toy with hole in the middle (or use a rawhide doughnut)

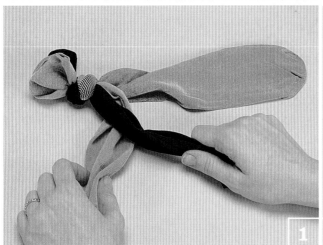

step one | Lay three stockings on your work surface. Arrange them so that two have the open end at the top and the third is the reverse, toe end up. Tie the three ends together in an overhand knot and then tightly braid the stockings together. Stop braiding about halfway through the length of the stockings.

step two | Separate one stocking from the braid and thread it through a cornstarch chew toy. Then continue braiding the length of the stockings. Finish by securing the three ends with another overhand knot. If you'd like to place more than one toy on the rope, separate two different stockings to thread through the toys, once at the beginning of the braid and then again near the end.

Squeaky Squirrel

Oh, those furry critters! If your dog loves the thrill of the chase, the embedded squeakers will encourage him to play. The generous tail also makes it perfect for the quieter dog that likes to carry and sleep with a favorite stuffed animal.

materials list

¼ yard (23cm) plush or fake fur remnants or scraps

fiberfill

two squeakers

Mylar sheets or general-purpose polyester film (optional)

white thread

scissors

straight pins

sewing machine and white thread

dull pencil

tapestry needle

sewing needle

patterns (page 83)

Pick Your Pattern

FOR A SMALLER DOG, USE THE CHIPMUNK PATTERNS ON PAGE 83. BOTH ANIMALS ARE CONSTRUCTED THE SAME WAY. SELECT THE PATTERN SIZE THAT FITS YOUR PET TO CREATE THE PERFECT CUSTOM-MADE PLUSH TOY.

step one | Use the patterns as your guide to cut two layers of plush fur for the tail and the body. Pin the wrong sides together and machine stitch around the body, starting where the tail will be attached. Finish stitching 1½" (4cm) from where you started. This will leave a large enough opening to turn the fabric right side out and later insert the tail end. Machine stitch around the tail, leaving the base unsewn. Turn both the stitched body and tail right side out. If necessary use a dull pencil point to help poke the small ears, feet and tail right side out. Use a tapestry needle point to pull trapped fur fibers free of the seam.

step two | Begin stuffing both pieces with fiberfill, stuffing the small places first. Continue stuffing until both pieces are halfway filled, and then place a squeaker into each piece. Cover the squeakers with additional fiberfill until both pieces are completely stuffed. (Optional: For a crinkle noise, you can stuff the tail with crumpled Mylar sheets.)

step three | Insert the tail end into the opening in the body and then hand sew the tail to the body.

Kitty Teaser

This interchangeable cat toy will challenge your cat's natural prey instincts. Attach either the swishing feathers or leather strips (shown on page 23) to the elastic end. When you grab the rod, you'll be entertained by your cat's dance to catch the swirling bait.

(shown on page 23)

materials list

21" (53cm) standard air-line tubing (sold with aquarium supplies)

29" (74cm) beading cord elastic

18" (46cm) dowel rod, 1/8" (3mm) diameter

electrical tape

size 5 black barrel swivel with interlocking snap (sold with fishing supplies)

striped foam ball (sold with cat toys)

five feathers

8" (20cm) beading cord elastic

scissors

glue gun

step one | Thread 29" (74cm) of beading cord elastic through the tubing so that the majority of the excess elastic extends below the tubing and several inches extend above the tubing.

step two | Insert all but 1" (3cm) of the dowel rod into the tubing alongside the elastic, making sure not to push the short elastic end back into the tube. The tubing will strengthen and protect the dowel rod and help prevent the long elastic end from knotting while in play.

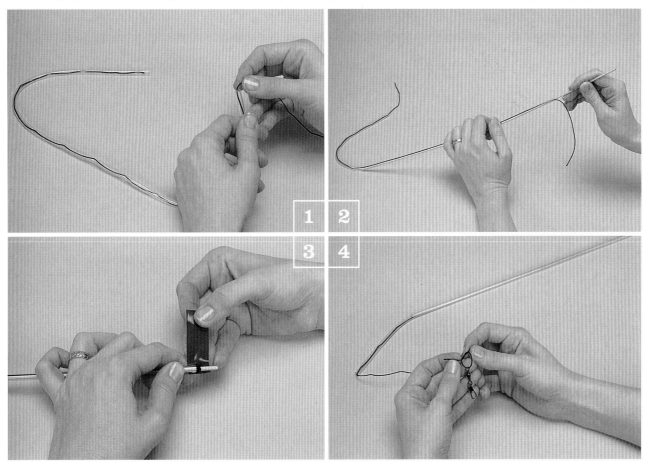

step three | Knot the short elastic end around the exposed dowel rod end and wrap a small piece of electrical tape around the end of the tubing to secure the knotted elastic.

step four | Thread and knot the long elastic end through one side of the barrel swivel. The other end of the barrel will connect the interchangeable toys to the finished rod.

step five | Use gentle pressure to push scissors points (substitute a pencil point when working with younger children) into a foam ball to make a ½" (1cm) deep hole.

step six | Tie five feather ends together with one end of an 8" (20cm) piece of elastic. Squeeze a generous drop of hot glue into the pierced hole and then firmly push the joined feather ends into the glue.

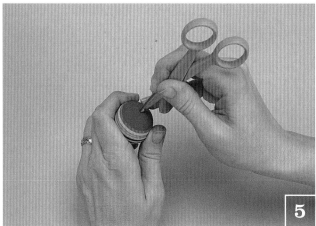

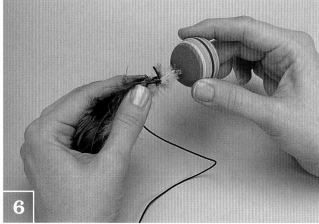

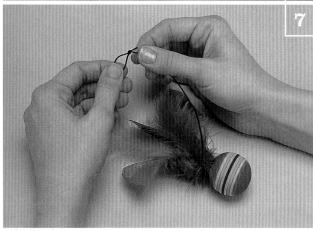

step seven | To attach the finished toy to the rod, thread and knot the extended elastic end into the other side of the barrel swivel.

Suede Tassel

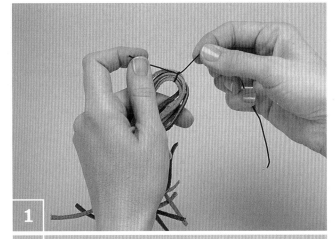

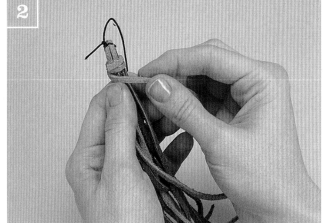

Durable Tassel Attachment

If flying feathers isn't your thing, try this suede tassel. It's stronger and your cat will think it is just as fun!

step one | Fold six suede laces in half and then knot one end of an 8" (20cm) piece of elastic around the centerfold of all six laces.

MATERIALS: Six 14" (36cm) suede laces • 8" (20cm) beading cord elastic • one 6" (15cm) suede lace

step two | Apply some hot glue just below the fold and place one end of a 6" (15cm) suede lace into the glue. Tightly wrap the length of the 6" (15cm) lace four times around the folded laces. Trim and secure the end against the laces with another drop of hot glue.

Squeaky Sock Snakes

Does your dog steal your socks? If so, this is the perfect toy for him. Save your odd socks and then fill them with squeakers and stuffing to make this charming toy. Don't be surprised if the finished sock snake trails behind your pet. It's sssso long.

materials list

four socks (size 9–11)

fiberfill

two squeakers (minimum)

white and tan yarn

felt scraps (two 2" x 1¼" [5cm x 3cm] wide ovals for eyes and 6" x 2" [15cm x 5cm] wide strip for tongue)

white thread

two 1" (25mm) pom-poms

clear, nontoxic craft glue (I used Aleene's Clear Gel Tacky Glue)

darning needle

sewing needle

Gluing Tip

WHEN GLUING SMALL ITEMS LIKE THE POM-POM EYES, USE STRAIGHT PINS TO HOLD THEM IN PLACE WHILE THE GLUE DRIES. BUT DON'T FORGET TO REMOVE THE PINS BEFORE PLAY.

step one | Starting with the sock that will become the snake's head, fill the toe (nose) with fiberfill and then insert the first squeaker. Cover the squeaker and fill the rest of the sock with more stuffing. Stuff the second sock and then insert it, toe end first, into the cuff of the head sock. Repeat this process for the third sock and insert it into the second sock.

step two | The last sock will become the snake's tail end. Stuff it partway and then insert the second squeaker. Cover the squeaker and fill the rest of the sock with more fiberfill. Fold the sock cuff over the filled sock and insert it, cuff end first, into the cuff of the third sock.

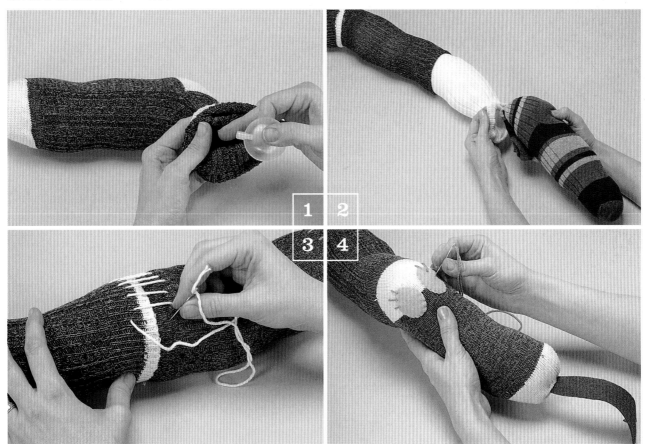

step three | Thread the darning needle with yarn and make 1" (3cm) long stitches where the socks overlap between the head and second socks, second and third socks, and third and tail end socks. When finished, cut two 2" (5cm) ovals and one 6" x 2" (15cm x 5cm) wide strip from felt scraps. Notch one end of the strip.

step four | With a sewing needle and thread, stitch the notched strip to the toe end of the sock head for the tongue. Next, stitch the two ovals to the heel of the sock for the eyes. Use the darning needle and yarn to make three 1/2" (1cm) stitches on top of each eye for eyelashes. Glue a pom-pom to the bottom of each felt eye.

Springy Snake

To make the finished pom-pom snakes irresistible, place them in a mason jar, sprinkle in a little catnip and shake. Decorate a colored paper circle with stamped paw prints along with the words *Catnip Critters* and then place it between the two-part metal lid.

   When your cats are ready to play, stretch the snakes between your fingertips to launch them across the room. They're guaranteed not to slither, but with a little help from your cat, they might turn up in unexpected places.

materials list

10" (25cm) thin beading cord elastic

ten to fourteen 1/4"–1" (6mm–25mm) pom-poms (purchase a bag full of assorted sizes and colors)

1" (3cm) maroon felt scrap (for tongue)

two small black pom-poms

clear, nontoxic craft glue (I used Aleene's Clear Gel Tacky Glue)

tapestry needle (necessary because it has a wide enough eye to accommodate the elastic and a sharp enough point to penetrate the center of the pom-pom)

scissors

step one | Thread the thin beading cord elastic through the needle and make a generous knot at the end. Starting with smaller pom-poms for the snake's tail end, pierce the needle through the center of the pom-poms and then slide them down the length of the elastic until they reach the knot. Alternate bright and dark pom-poms while increasing their size as you work your way along your snake's body. When you've made a snake that is ten to fourteen pom-poms long, end with the largest pom-pom for the head.

step two | Cut a 1" (3cm) forked tongue out of a felt scrap. Pierce the needle through the flat end of the felt tongue and slide it up against the pom-pom head. Knot the elastic several times against the tongue and then trim the end.

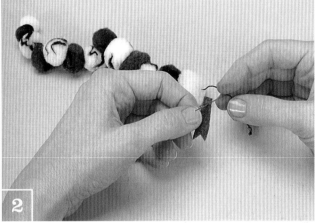

1 2 3

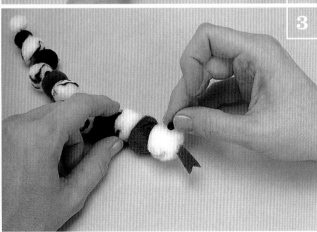

step three | Use clear, nontoxic craft glue to glue two small black pom-pom eyes onto either side of the pom-pom head. Separate the pom-pom fuzz with your fingertips to create an opening to set each eye deep into the head.

Tennis Ball Launcher

materials list

24" (61cm) of $3/8$" (1cm) wide elastic

standard-size tennis ball

scissors

clear, nontoxic craft glue (I used Aleene's Clear Gel Tacky Glue)

Taking only minutes to make, this toy is perfect for the dog or cat who likes to chase and retrieve. The cat version is small enough to use indoors. You'll want a big open space to launch the larger dog version of this toy. Hook it through your belt loop and head to the park.

Playing Tip

HOLD THE HANDLE IN YOUR FINGERTIPS AND LASSO IT IN CIRCLES ABOVE YOUR HEAD BEFORE LAUNCHING IT ACROSS LARGE OPEN SPACES. YOU CAN ALSO HOLD IT BETWEEN TWO HANDS AND PULL BACK ON IT TO INCREASE TENSION, LAUNCHING IT LIKE A LARGE ELASTIC BAND. SMALLER DOGS WILL PREFER TO CARRY THE BALL BACK TO YOU BY ITS HANDLE.

For Cats, Too

CATS LOVE THE TENNIS BALL LAUNCHER, TOO! USE A SMALL 2" (5CM) TENNIS BALL AND $1/8$" (3MM) ELASTIC AND FOLLOW THE DIRECTIONS ON PAGE 29.

step one | Lay the length of the elastic on your work surface and position the ball at two-thirds of the elastic's length. This uneven placement will provide added length on one side of the elastic to later become the handle. Pull the uneven ends up the sides of the ball. Tightly cross them where they meet at the top of the tennis ball. Wrap the elastic back down the sides of the ball. Tightly knot the ends together where they cross over the first wrapping.

step two | Create the looped handle by threading the very end of the long elastic end under both the wrapped and tied elastic. Tightly knot it a second time to the short end and then trim the ends.

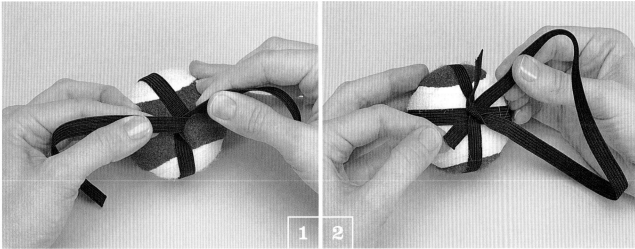

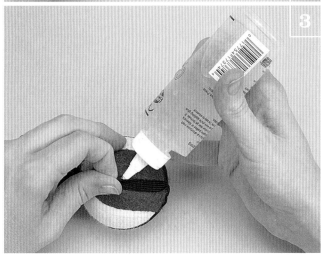

step three | Lift one small section of elastic at a time to apply clear, nontoxic craft glue between the ball and elastic. This added step will help prevent the ball from slipping out of its elastic sling. Apply more glue to strengthen the knots and stop the ends from fraying. Let the glue dry overnight before play.

PET ACCESSORIES

The accessories chapter has everything a pet could want, from puffy pillow beds to treat canisters. All these great projects are beautiful, functional and easy to make. Pampering your pet has never been so much fun!

As pet lovers, we've all done some creative things to give our pets good lives, and some pets demand a little more creative thinking on our part, especially if the pet has had bad experiences.

Tim was a stray cat before he came to my parents' home. He approached every meal as if it were his last. He used to gobble his food so quickly that he would inevitably get sick. After some creative thinking, my mother decided to hand-feed him his morning and evening snacks to slow him down. She sat down and threw pieces of dry food one at a time onto the carpet in front of him. Timmy played along, moving from one piece to another, but he soon grew impatient for the food to land, so he tried catching the pieces in midair. Successful, he refined his technique by sitting up on his back haunches and catching the food in his mouth or with his front paws. My mum delights in his performance, and I think he ends up with more food for the added effort.

Tim the Food Catcher

materials list

shrink-art plastic (I used Aleene's Shrink-It)

jewelry glue (I used Aleene's Platinum Bond Glass & Bead Slick Surfaces Adhesive)

eyelet charm with ⅛" (3mm) opening (sold in a multiple-size package)

small rhinestones

split ring (sold in a multiple-size package)

pencil

2" (5cm) diameter jar lid

scissors

oven

black fine-point permanent marker

gold metallic paint marker (optional)

Vanity Tags

If it just isn't enough to have your pet's name and city license tags hanging from her collar, this is the perfect project for you. With a little shrink-art material, metal tags and a few rhinestones, you can make personalized collar jewelry.

step one | Lightly pencil a 2" (5cm) circle (use a small jar lid as a pattern) onto the shrink-art plastic sheet and then cut it out. Use a black permanent marker to write a name or message onto the center of the disk. If you wish, adorn the tag with a small drawing made with a gold metallic paint marker. Shrink the decorated tag in a preheated oven as instructed on the package of shrink-art plastic.

step two | Use jewelry glue to attach the shrunk plastic below the punched hole in the metal eyelet, then glue a rhinestone to the shrunk plastic. Use a split ring to attach the tag to a collar.

1 2

They're So Vain
Even finicky felines will appreciate the attention a vanity tag will bring. The cat versions are made the same way as the dog's, just select smaller eyelets and begin with a 1¼" (3cm) circle of shrink-art plastic.

Puffy Pet Pillows

Like the princess and the pea, even the most discerning cat or dog will appreciate the warmth and softness of these beds. Iron-on appliqués and tied layers of fleece will reward nonsewers with a showpiece upholstered pet bed elegant enough for a place of honor in your living room.

materials list

two 28" (71cm) fleece squares, one solid and the other patterned

fusible web for heavyweight fabrics (I used Heat n Bond Ultrahold)

fleece scrap (for appliqué)

reddish brown and golden brown embroidery floss

20" (51cm) pillow

fabric shears

yardstick

iron

tapestry needle

pattern (page 84)

Large Pillows

FOR LARGER HAND-TIED PILLOWS, CUT THE FLEECE 8" (20CM) LONGER THAN THE HEIGHT AND WIDTH OF THE PILLOW YOU PLAN TO USE. THIS WILL ENSURE THAT YOU'LL HAVE ENOUGH FABRIC FOR 4" (10CM) LONG STRIPS ON ALL FOUR SIDES OF THE PILLOW. THE OTHER VARIATION WILL BE THE EXTRA 1" (3CM) WIDE STRIPS THE ADDED LENGTH AND WIDTH WILL CREATE ON EACH SIDE OF THE PILLOW.

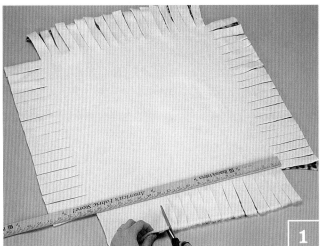

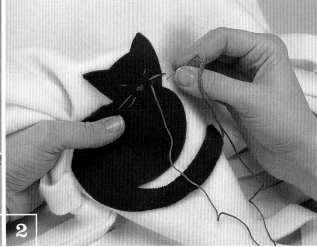

1 **2** **3**

step one | Stack the two fleece squares together and then cut 4" (10cm) squares out each corner. Place the yardstick along one side of the pillow cover, resting it against the top edge of the cut openings. Cut 1" (3cm) wide strips up to the edge of the yardstick. Each strip should be 4" (10cm) long. Continue working in this fashion until you've cut a total of twenty 1" (3cm) strips along each side of the pillow cover. Next, follow the label directions to adhere the fusible web to the back of the fleece scrap. Trace the cat (or dog) pattern (see page 84) onto the paper backing of the applied web. Cut out the cat and peel off the paper backing. Follow the label directions to bond the fleece cat to one corner of the solid fleece pillow cover.

step two | Use the entire thickness of embroidery floss to stitch the cat's face. With the reddish brown floss, make a single diagonal stitch for each eye and a series of small stitches to form a triangular nose. Use golden brown floss to make two long stitches for whiskers on either side of the nose. Tie all floss knots on the back side of the pillow cover.

step three | Place the pillow between the two fleece pillow covers, making sure the cat appliqué faces out. Match the bottom and top cover strips at the corners and knot them first. Continue knotting the top and bottom strips together around all four sides until the pillow is completely concealed.

Large Dog Bed

The Perfect Pet Bed
This more practical pillow cover for animals that enjoy the great outdoors can be easily removed for washing.

materials list

33" (84cm) solid fleece square

fusible web for heavy-weight fabrics (I used Heat n Bond Ultrahold)

fleece scraps (for appliqué)

embroidery floss

33" x 23" (84cm x 58cm) and 33" x 16" (84cm x 41cm) sections of patterned fleece

30" (76cm) pillow

fabric shears

iron

tapestry needle

straight pins

sewing machine and white thread

pattern (page 84)

step one | On the solid fleece square, apply the dog appliqué and embroider the face (see steps 1 and 2, page 35), creating an upside-down Y-shaped mouth instead of whiskers. Position the finished cover right side up on your work surface. Arrange the two patterned fleece sections right sides down over the cover so that the pieces overlap for 6" (15cm) at the off-center opening. Pin the edges together and then machine stitch around all four sides. Pull the cover right side out through the back opening. Stuff the pillow between the two back pieces. They'll overlap to conceal the pillow.

Paw Wipe

Pawse before you enter! Hang this handy towel by your door to stop those muddy paw prints from covering your floors.

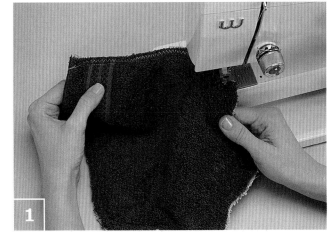

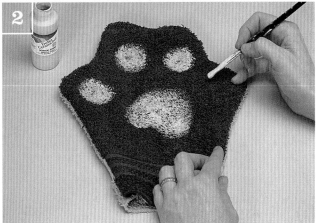

MATERIALS: two washcloths (different shades) • acrylic paint • ½-inch (13mm) flat paintbrush • straight pins • scissors • sewing machine and white thread • pattern (page 84)

step one | Stack the washcloths right sides together, matching the finished edges. Pin the pattern through both cloths, aligning the bottom opening of the mitt with the finished edges of the washcloths. Cut the cloths, then remove the pattern and repin the cloths together. Machine stitch around the mitt, leaving the bottom open. Using a zigzag setting, machine stitch a second time along the outside edge to prevent fraying. Turn the mitt right sides out.

step two | Use a dry paint brush and acrylic paint to brush a paw pattern on one side of the finished mitt.

Trimmed Collar & Leash

Fabric-Trimmed Leash

Why settle for regular collars and leashes or spend a small fortune on designer sets when they're affordable and fun to decorate yourself? Use this technique to add any kind of trim to plain collars and leashes.

materials list

leash

collar

1–2 yard (1m–2m) strip of fabric trim (trim varies with the length of the collar and leash handle; look for trim that is thinner than the width of the collar/leash)

fabric glue (I used Fabri-Tac)

scissors

step one | Lay the trim over the collar to establish the desired length and then cut it accordingly. Thread one end of the cut trim under the plastic buckle at the center of the collar. Draw the trim through the buckle and then center it over the top of the collar. Squeeze a small amount of fabric glue between the trim and collar in the center of the buckle. Next, glue both edges of the trim to the collar. Measure a second length of trim to cover the leash handle. Glue the cut trim around the handle. Finally, apply a bead of glue to the cut ends on both the collar and leash to prevent fraying.

Decorating Tips

1. PREWASH BOTH THE COLLAR AND LEASH TO REMOVE THE SIZING. SIZING IS PLACED ON THE FABRIC DURING MANUFACTURING AND WILL INTERFERE WITH THE GLUE'S ABILITY TO BOND.

2. ADJUST THE WASHED COLLAR TO A COMFORTABLE FIT FOR YOUR PET BEFORE DECORATING.

3. ALLOW THE GLUE TO DRY FOR 24 HOURS TO FIRMLY SET BEFORE USE.

Sweet as a Rose Collar & Leash

Arrange ribbon roses in a line along the center top of the collar and under the leash's handle. Once you're pleased with the arrangement, glue the ribbon roses in place with fabric glue.

Rhinestone Collar & Leash

All eyes will be on your pet when she steps out wearing a rhinestone-studded collar and leash ensemble. Use this technique to set any kind of rhinestone shape into the collar and leash.

Safety Tip

FREQUENTLY CHECK TO MAKE SURE THE RHINESTONES ARE SECURE. RUN YOUR FINGERS OVER THE BACK OF THE COLLAR TO ENSURE THE PRONGS ARE SAFELY BENT INTO THE FABRIC AWAY FROM YOUR PET'S SKIN.

materials list

leash

collar

Gem-Tac

rhinestone daisies

rhinestone setter or flathead screwdriver (I used the BeDazzler Custom Hand Tool)

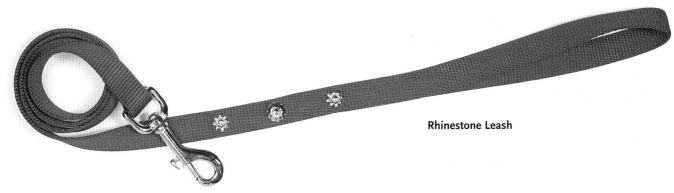

Rhinestone Leash

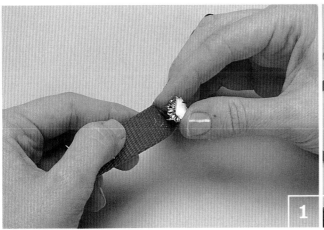

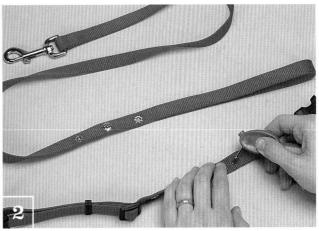

1 | 2

step one | Working on the right side of the collar, squeeze a small amount of Gem-Tac into the back of a rhinestone and then push it through the thickness of the collar (place rhinestones only where the collar is a single thickness).

step two | Flip the collar over and then use a rhinestone setter or a flathead screwdriver to bend the metal prongs back down into the material. If you have difficulty getting the prongs to fully push through, apply pressure to the front of the rhinestone or press it firmly against a hard work surface. Continue working, setting one rhinestone at a time, to create a repeated arrangement of studs in both the collar and leash. Run your fingers over the back to make sure it is smooth and all the prongs are bent back into the fabric. For your pet's safety, repeat the smoothness check whenever you remove the collar.

Chow Time Bowls & Place Mats

Personalized ceramic pet dishes can be expensive. I found that simply decorated pasta, cereal, soup or small mixing bowls make affordable and practical alternatives. Pair them with graphic no-slip place mats for an easy-to-clean elegant pet dining area.

materials list

Bowls:

white ceramic bowls

water-based ceramic pen (I used Pébéo: Porcelaine 150)

vinegar

paper towels

oven

Place Mats:

black craft foam sheet

brown or black paint marker (I used a brown DecoColor paint marker)

CraftFoam Glue

cork place mats (substitute a full craft foam sheet if you can't locate a cork mat)

scissors

standard hole punch

pattern (page 85)

Pick Your Pattern

FOR THE PLACE MATS, CHOOSE FROM FISH, BONE AND HEART PATTERNS ON PAGE 85 TO CREATE THE PERFECT DINING AREA FOR YOUR PET.

step one | Remove any labels and prewash the bowls in hot soapy water. Rinse them in diluted vinegar to remove any oily fingerprints. Dry the bowls completely with paper towels while holding them by the rim and base to avoid making new fingerprints on the drawing area. Using a water-based ceramic pen, write your pet's name or a cute saying on the front of the bowls. Once you're pleased with your design, place the bowls in a preheated oven to cure according to the ceramic pen instructions. If you make a mistake, wash it off the bowl with soap and water, dry and then try again. The ink is not permanent until after it is baked.

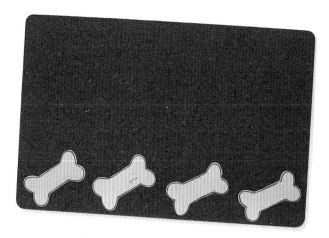

Doggie Dining

Use the ceramic pen to draw your dog's face with a bone in his mouth on one bowl and then write *Bone Appétit* on the other bowl. Bake according to package directions. Use the dog bone pattern (see page 85) to cut out tan craft foam bones and glue them to a black cork mat with CraftFoam Glue.

step two | Cut four fish shapes out of black craft foam (see pattern on page 85). Use the hole punch to make an eyehole in each craft foam fish. Use a brown paint marker to outline the eyehole and outside edge of each fish. Use CraftFoam glue to attach each fish on the diagonal in a line across the bottom of the cork mat. Let the glue dry completely before using the place mat.

Treat Canisters

materials list

copper and terra-cotta polymer clay (I used Sculpey III polymer clay)

plastic alphabet beads

clear round acrylic (or glass) canisters

jewelry glue (I used Aleene's Platinum Bond Glass & Bead Slick Surfaces Adhesive)

glass baking dish

fiberfill

oven

masking tape

Whether your dog begs for bones or your cat flips for fish, goodies from the treat jar are what they're after. Make a container worthy of all the attention it receives. Personalize the treat canister with names and messages embedded in bone- or fish-shaped polymer clay pieces. You might be surprised at how many humans appreciate your decorative efforts, as well.

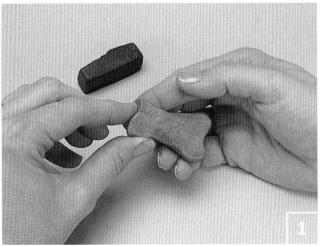

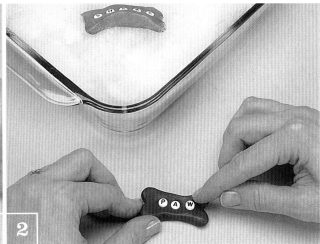

step one | Use the natural division lines in the clay to measure a single bar for the small bones and two bars to make a large bone. Use your fingertips to compress the ends of the clay bars into indented bone ends. Smooth both the sides and ends to give the finished bone an allover rounded appearance.

step two | Spelling out a dog message, arrange the letters on top of the bone, separating them by at least 1/8" (3mm). Press them one at a time into the bone. If necessary, smooth the clay around the embedded beads to fill any gaps that might allow the beads to shift. Mold each finished bone onto a side of the canister so that it bends to match the contour of the surface.

Carefully lay the curved bones in a glass baking dish lined with fiberfill. The cushioning will allow the bones to retain their shape when baking. Cure the bones in a preheated oven according to package directions. Apply jewelry glue to the underside of one bone at a time. Use a long strip of masking tape to hold the bones in place against the canister while the glue dries.

Cat Treat Canister
Start with a smaller canister. Shape lavender and turquoise polymer clay into fish with your fingertips. Embed beads into the fish to spell out cat messages. Follow the dog instructions to mold, cure and adhere the fish to the canister. Fill the finished canister with your cat's favorite treats.

FOR KIDS
WHO LOVE PETS

While most of this book is dedicated to the pets in our lives, this chapter is devoted to the kids who love pets. These projects are perfect for family crafting or gift giving, and pet lovers of all ages will enjoy these projects.

Pets are a special part of our lives, bringing joy (and surprises) every day. My sons, Jasper and Elliot, have a special bond with Maizy, our wheaten terrier, and Maizy has a unique way of showing that she cares. She steals their left shoes!

One Saturday morning when we were leaving for our younger son Elliot's soccer game, we realized his left cleat was missing. We checked all over the house but couldn't find the cleat. On Monday morning just as the boys were getting ready for school, we realized that Elliot's left running shoe was missing. We searched the house a second time and came up empty-handed again. The next day Elliot's left sandal disappeared. We pulled apart his room, and buried deep in a chest of stuffed animals, we found both the cleat and the running shoe. In our older son Jasper's room we found the missing sandal nestled in a trunk of clothes.

I wish we could catch Maizy in the act. I think it's her way of taking care of the boys while they are gone.

Maizy the Left-Shoe Thief

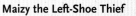

47

Sassy Cat Costume

These costume accessories are so easy to make that they'll solve any dress-up dilemma in minutes. The soft feathered boas come in a myriad of colors and ripple with the slightest of movements. Add a turtleneck, leggings and a little face paint, and you're sure to take first prize in any costume contest.

materials list

gray stiffened felt (for backing)

colored felt

1" (3cm) fabric covered head-band (no teeth)

two 2-yard (2m) boas, one dark multicolored and one white or light colored

scissors

glue gun or Kids Choice Glue

pattern (page 85)

step one | Cut the ear pattern out of both the stiffened felt and colored felt. Glue the two colored felt ears over the stiffened felt ears. Glue the base of each ear to the top of the headband, leaving 2½"–3" (6cm–7cm) between them.

step two | Cut an 18" (46cm) section from the multicolored boa. Turn the headband over and glue the boa piece to the back side of the headband. Start gluing at the base of one ear and work around the entire ear, over the top of the headband and then around the second ear.

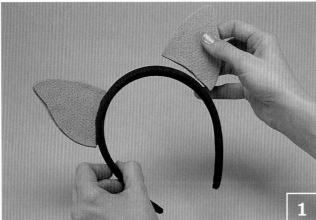 

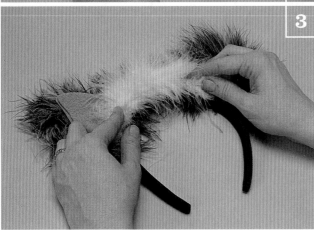

step three | Cut a 6" (15cm) section from the white boa. Turn the headband over and glue the white boa section between the two ears, centered on the front of the headband. Use the remaining length of the dark multicolored boa for a tail. Loop one end around a belt loop or safety pin it under the back of a shirt.

Top Dog

For a dog costume, cut the dog ear pattern (see page 85) out of black felt. Edge the ears with a section of black boa, then add bangs with a small piece of black and gray multicolored boa. Fold the remaining black and gray boa in half to make a thick dog tail. Hot glue the layers together and then pin the ends under the back of a shirt.

materials list

prepackaged 5½" x 4 (14cm x 10cm) tan and red folded note cards (or substitute 5½" x 8" [14cm x 20cm] colored paper sheets, folded in half)

5½" x 8" (14cm x 20cm) corrugated cardboard, folded in half

scrapbook paper

metal-rimmed circle tags

scissors

black fine-point permanent marker

craft glue

⅛" (3mm) hole punch

string

Pet Pop-Ups

Surprise your friends with these clever cards. One simple cut and fold makes the cat or dog "speak" a heartfelt message. The addition of a personalized pet tag and scrapbook paper collar adds style to these fun-filled cards.

Gluing Tip

WHEN GLUING, LAY THE CARD FLAT, SO WHEN THE CARD IS OPENED, IT WILL OPEN ALL THE WAY.

Starting at the folded edge of the tan card, make a smile-shaped cut through both layers of the card 1½" (4cm) from the bottom edge. Lift the bottom portion of the smile up and fold it down toward the card's outside edge. Run your fingertips down the length of the fold to form crease lines. Unfold it and push the jowls inside the card. Open and close the card to test the pop-up.

step two | Lay the card flat and use a black permanent marker to draw a heart-shaped nose and three whisker spots on either side of the nose. Draw two circular eyes on the outer crease lines and a half-circle chin under the pop-up mouth. Outline the dog's head: Start at one end of the cut line, work up the side of the head around one ear, over the top of the head, around the second ear, and down the other side of the head, and end at the other end of the cut line.

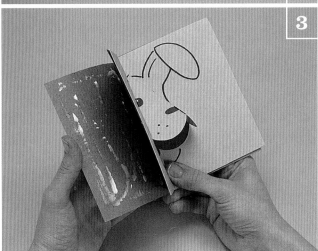

step three | Glue the back of the tan card to the inside of the red card, taking care not to put any glue on the jowl area between the creases that will prevent it from popping. Then glue the back of the red card to the inside of the corrugated cardboard.

51

4

step four | Cut and glue a scrapbook paper collar under the dog's chin. Use a ⅛" (3mm) hole punch to punch a small hole through all the paper layers on one side of the collar. Remove the small metal split ring from the tag and thread a piece of string through the hole in the tag. Then thread the string ends through the punched hole and knot the ends on the back of the card to prevent the tag from falling out.

Happy Birthday Pop-Up

To make the terrier version, draw elongated zig-zags to give the illusion of long shaggy fur. End the ears in a point and write a birthday message on the tag.

Cat Pop-Ups

To make the cat cards, draw the eyes below the fold lines and make two pointed ears at the top of the head. Draw two or three long whiskers on either side of the nose. For a striped cat (shown at left), make V-shaped lines at the top and sides of the head. For a long-haired cat (shown at bottom), outline the face and ears with loose zigzag lines.

materials list

¼ yard (23cm) each of light gray and black fleece (for a solid colored pet, use ¼ yard [23cm] of fleece)

fiberfill

polypropylene pellets

black thread

dark gray fleece scraps

black embroidery floss

two ⅝" (2cm) yellow buttons

scissors

straight pins

sewing machine and white thread

sewing needle

tapestry needle

patterns (page 86 and 87)

Sewing Tip

USE A DULL PENCIL POINT TO HELP TURN SMALL AREAS, SUCH AS THE FEET AND THE END OF THE TAIL, RIGHT SIDE OUT.

Fleece Friends

Soft and floppy, these fleece felines and canines (see page 57) are sure to spread smiles. Fleece is the perfect **fabric for beginning sewers. It's easy to cut and stitch and** doesn't fray. All the pets are constructed the same way. Just change the fabric colors and the head, ear and tail patterns to customize your fleece friend.

step one | Cut two layers of contrasting fabric for the head, body and tail patterns. Stack each set right sides together and then pin and machine stitch them together, leaving the base of the tail open and a 1" (3cm) opening on both the side of the head and one of the body's legs.

step two | Turn each of the three pieces right side out through the openings. Stuff the head and tail pieces with fiberfill. Stuff the feet with fiberfill and then add pellets to fill the remainder of the body. Use a sewing needle and black thread to hand stitch the body and head openings closed, but leave the tail open.

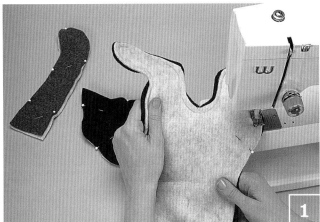
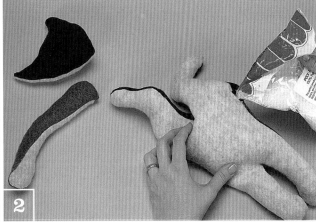
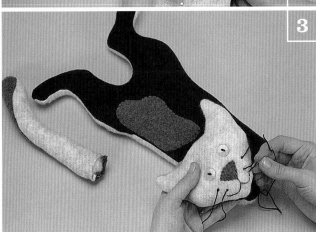

step three | Cut a spot and nose from dark gray fleece scraps. Hand stitch the spot onto the back of the body and the nose onto the face with black thread. Thread the tapestry needle with the entire thickness of black embroidery floss and stitch the two button eyes above the nose. Make a single 1/2" (1cm) stitch down from the bottom of the nose and then make two more 1/2" (1cm) stitches on either side for the mouth. For the first set of whiskers, make a knot 2 1/2" (6cm) from the end of the floss and then push the needle from one side of the jowls to the other. Pull the thread all the way through. Knot the floss where it comes back out of the fleece and then trim the end 2 1/2" (6cm) from the knot. Repeat the process to make the second set of whiskers.

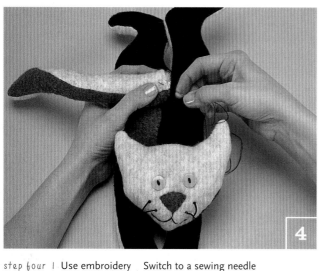

step four | Use embroidery floss to connect the center back of the head to the body. Center it above the paws. Let the head remain somewhat movable to add character.

Switch to a sewing needle and black thread to hand stitch around the base of the tail to join it to the back of the body.

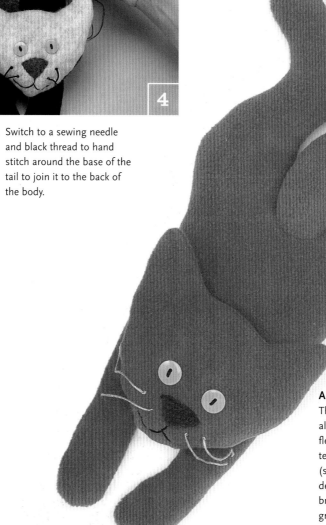

A Cat of a Different Color
The marmalade cat is made almost entirely with orange fleece. Use the variation patterns for the head and tail (see page 86), tan embroidery floss for the whiskers, brown fleece for the nose and green buttons for the eyes.

Making Popular Pups

Cut and sew all pieces the same as the cat except for the following two alterations: For the body, leave an opening between the legs (instead of on the side of a leg) and then insert and hand stitch the stuffed tail into the opening in the stuffed body. When machine stitching the head, leave 1" (3cm) openings at the top of the head where the ears will be placed (instead of the side of the head). Pin and machine stitch around two pairs of cut ears, leaving the bottom edge open. Turn the ears right side out and lightly stuff them with fiberfill to make them stick up or pellets if you want them to droop. Fold the bottom of the ears and insert and hand stitch each one into an opening in the stuffed head.

For the Labrador pup (near right), cut the head, ear, tail and body pattern pieces out of gray fleece. Cut the nose pattern out of black fleece. Make a wide upturned mouth to fill the larger jowl area and then stitch the orange button eyes in place.

To make the Chihuahua (far right), cut the face and body patterns out of camel-colored fleece. Cut a tail, nose and large spot out of brown fleece. Cut a second smaller spot out of white fleece. Hand stitch the spots onto the stuffed dog back and head before stitching on the gray/black button eyes.

Pet Pal Journals

Use soft felt and scrapbook papers to transform notebooks into one of these dog or cat books. Movable eyes, ribbons and whiskers add character to the cut pattern pieces, and the tail folds down to mark your place. You'll want to keep the finished journal by your bed to write diary entries. Make an extra book to record your pet's achievements, special friends, favorite games and funny moments.

materials list

7½" x 9¾" (19cm x 25cm) composition book

two pieces of 9" x 12" (23cm x 30cm) adhesive-backed felt (I used Presto Felt)

light and dark brown felt sheets

plush or fake fur scraps

craft glue or Kids Choice Glue

12" (30cm) of ribbon

adhesive felt dots (or cut out circles from felt)

movable plastic eyes

solid colored scrapbook papers

scissors

patterns (page 88)

Pick Your Pattern

TO MAKE A LITTLE KITTY OR PUPPY JOURNAL (SHOWN ON COVER), SIMPLY USE A SMALL 3½" X 4½" (9CM X 11CM) COMPOSITION BOOK, REFER TO THE VARIATION PATTERNS ON PAGE 88, AND FOLLOW THE BASIC DIRECTIONS ON PAGE 59. IT'S THAT EASY!

step one | Cover the front of the notebook with one piece of adhesive-backed felt, aligning the fabric with the outside edge of the binding. Cut off both corners of the felt, then fold down the top and bottom felt edges over the notebook. Fold the side edge down last. Repeat to cover the back of the notebook.

step two | Cut the face pattern pieces out of the light and dark brown felt and fake fur scraps. Arrange them over the notebook cover and glue them in place. Make a ribbon bow and glue it to the bottom of the notebook under the dog's chin. Press the felt dots above the nose and then glue plastic eyes on top of the felt dots.

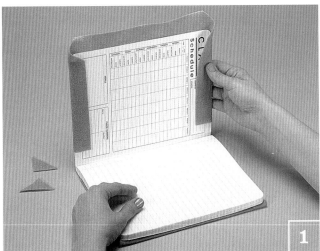

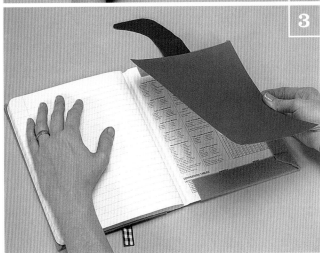

step three | Cut the tail pattern out of dark brown felt and glue the end of it to the top of the inside back cover. Cut two sheets of scrapbook paper 7¼" x 9½" (18cm x 24cm) and then glue one to the inside front cover and the other to the inside back cover. The paper conceals both the felt connections and the preprinted text.

materials list

plush fur scraps

white thread

fiberfill

pair of slippers (any size)

black embroidery floss

fabric glue (I used Fabri-Tac)

two medium-size brown pom-poms (for noses)

four small black and four tiny white pom-poms (for the eyes)

scissors

straight pins

sewing machine and white thread

sewing needle

tapestry needle

pattern (page 89)

Kitten Slippers

Kick off your shoes and slip your feet into a pair of fun furry slippers. Plush fur scraps and pom-poms turn plain slippers into a pair of kittens or puppies (see page 62). They're a snap to make, especially if you've already made the Fleece Friends (see page 54); the ear patterns and stitching are the same.

step one | Cut eight plush ears (see pattern on page 89) and then pair them right sides together. Pin the fabric layers together and machine stitch around all four ears, leaving the bottom edges open. Turn each ear right side out. Use a tapestry needle point to loosen any fur fibers trapped in the seam. Stuff each ear with fiberfill and then hand sew two ears to the top of each slipper.

step two | Using a tapestry needle and the entire thickness of black embroidery floss, stitch a mouth through the toe of each slipper. For the whiskers, knot the floss 2" (5cm) from the end and then stitch from one side of the slipper to the other. Pull the floss through so the knot holds the first whisker in place. Make a second knot where the floss comes back out through the slipper and then trim the floss 2" (5cm) from the knot. Repeat the process to make a second set of whiskers on the first slipper and two sets of whiskers on the second slipper.

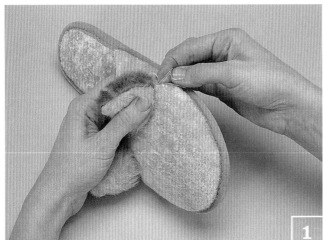

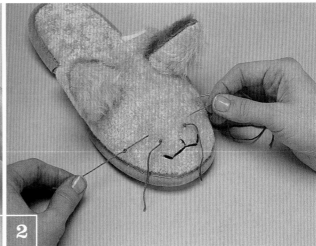

1 2

3

step three | Use fabric glue to attach a brown pom-pom nose and two black and white pom-pom eyes on each slipper. Push a straight pin down through the top white pom-poms on the eyes and the brown pom-pom noses to anchor them in place while the glue dries overnight. Remove all pins before wearing.

Puppy Slippers

Use the puppy pattern to cut eight ears out of plush fur and then follow the kitten directions to stitch the four pairs together and attach them to the slippers. Use the jowl pattern to cut two plush jowls and glue one to the front of each slipper. Glue a large pom-pom nose to the center of each jowl. For the gray dog (at right), you'll also need to cut four plush tails. Sew the two pairs together and stitch the tail ends to the heel of each slipper. Glue pom-pom eyes directly onto the slipper. To make the Dalmatian (at top), you'll also need to cut four white spots and glue a pair above the jowl and below the ears of each black slipper. Glue pom-pom eyes over the spots.

Cork Frame

Readily available cork tiles are a user-friendly, durable wood substitute. This quick and easy frame is made with a single tile.

MATERIALS: 6" x 6" (15cm x 15cm) cork tile • permanent black ink • metallic silver and black paper • craft glue • 4" x 6" (10cm x 15cm) photo • transparent tape • four self-adhesive double-sided tape strips (packaged with the cork tiles) • 6" x 6" (15cm x 15cm) piece of black posterboard • black duct tape • self-healing cutting board • craft knife • dog and alphabet stamps (see Resource Guide on page 94)

step one | Working on a cutting board, use a craft knife to cut a 3" x 5" (8cm x 13cm) opening in the cork tile. (Keep the rectangle to make the stand.) Stamp images and phrases onto silver paper. Layer the images onto black paper. Glue the stamped pieces underneath the opening. Working on the back side of the frame, position your photo facedown over the opening and tape it in place. Place self-adhesive double-sided tape strips on the four corners of the piece of black posterboard. Mount the frame and photo onto the prepared posterboard.

step two | Make a diagonal cut down the 3" x 5" (8cm x 13cm) piece of cork tile (left over from cutting the opening in step 1) to make two right-angle triangles. Use black duct tape to attach one triangle to the back of the frame for a stand. If necessary, loosen the duct tape strip to allow the cork triangle to swing open and closed.

Cork Photo Album

Get out your rubber stamp collection and personalize an album to coordinate with the frame on page 63. The decorative bead slides up and down the elastic to open and close the book.

Cat Photo Album

USE CAT STAMPS AND A CAT-RELATED PHRASE LIKE *CATNAPS* TO CENTER ON THE ALBUM. USE ADHESIVE PHOTO CORNERS TO MOUNT PHOTOS ONTO THE INSIDE PAGES. DECORATE AROUND THE PHOTOS WITH STAMPS AND STICKERS.

step one | Ink the dog stamp with black permanent ink and stamp it onto metallic silver paper. Inking one alphabet letter at a time, stamp *Good Dog* onto the silver paper, as well. Let the ink dry while you prepare the album covers.

step two | Protect your work surface with a cutting board. Using scissors, make a hole ³⁄₄" (2cm) from the left edge and ³⁄₄" (2cm) up from the bottom on one tile. Then make a second hole ³⁄₄" (2cm) from the left edge and ³⁄₄" (2cm) down from the top. Using an eyelet setter and small hammer, set an eyelet into each hole. Repeat the process to set a pair of eyelet holes in the second tile to make the back cover.

step three | Cut out the stamped images and phrases. Frame the stamped dog with a slightly larger rectangle of black paper and glue it along with the words to the center of the front cover. Position the cover over the interior paper sheets to mark the positioning of the holes with a pencil, then make two holes in each sheet with a hole punch. Stack the punched pages in between the cork covers. To assemble, thread the elastic cord down through the bottom hole, going from the front to the back cover. Then bring the cord up through the top hole of the back cover and through to the front. Thread both ends of the elastic through the center of the bead. The bead should slide with slight resistance up and down the elastic cords, adjusting to allow the book to open freely or close tightly. Trim the ends of the cord and then dab the cut ends with glue to avoid fraying.

PET
CELEBRATIONS

If you're up to the challenge of hosting a pet party, you'll find party hats, gifts and card ideas here. The quick and easy Halloween costumes, Christmas stockings and keepsake ornaments will celebrate your pet through the seasons.

We celebrate Maizy's birthday every year. Our celebrations always start with a cake from the dog bakery, and once every crumb has been eaten, the games begin. Maizy takes her role as hostess very seriously and initiates a game of tug-of-war by holding a branch in her mouth and prancing around until one or two of the other dogs grab the ends. Hide-and-seek is another favorite, and the final game of the day is fetch. The dogs race to the end of the yard in an attempt to be the first to catch and keep the ball away from the other dogs. Needless to say, the dogs leave well fed and well exercised. We even give the guests goody bags to take home, because what's a party without leftovers!

Maizy the Party Dog

Treat Gift Cards

This little card is the perfect topper to a treat-filled dish, or it can be a gift in and of itself. Use the same technique and just change the color of the scrapbook paper to make a card for any season—green paper with red ribbon for Christmas or orange and black ribbon for Halloween.

materials list

scrapbook paper

¼" (6mm) wide ribbon

fur-covered mouse (sold with cat toys)

self-healing cutting board

craft knife

fine-tipped black marker

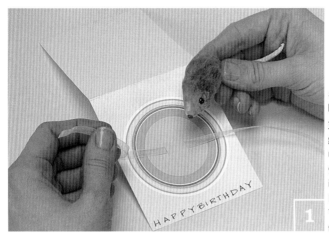

step one | Cut the scrapbook paper into an 8½" x 3½" (22cm x 9cm) rectangle, and then fold it in half to measure 4¼" x 3½" (11cm x 9cm). Open the card and lay it flat on the cutting board. Make two ¼" (6mm) slits ½" (1cm) apart centered on the front of the card. Draw the ribbon down through one slit, across the underside of the front cover and back up through the second slit. Wrap the ribbon ends around the mouse and tie them in a bow. Use a fine-tipped black marker to write a birthday message on the card cover.

Dog Birthday Card

For a doggone good treat, tie a biscuit to the front of the card. (But do not tie the bone in place too far in advance, because the oils from the baked bone can leach out into the paper.) You can substitute small rawhide and specialty chew bones. For larger bones, increase the size of the card and add a second set of cuts along with a second ribbon to hold the additional length in place.

Birthday Bowls

Pet birthdays spread smiles. Don't let your pet's big day pass without a party. If you're invited to a celebration, don't just bring treats in a gift bag. These plastic bowls can be purchased for a couple of dollars and customized in minutes. Coupled with a quick and easy treat card (see page 68), the filled bowl will delight both the owner and pet.

(see page 68)

materials list

plastic food and water bowls

yellow and white broad-tipped paint markers (I used DecoColor paint markers)

tan and blue fine-tipped paint markers (I used DecoColor paint markers)

Mistakes Happen

IT'S NOT THE END OF THE WORLD IF YOU MAKE A MISTAKE. USE GOO GONE TO WIPE OFF THE MARKER WITH A PAPER TOWEL AND START OVER.

step one | Use a yellow broad-tipped paint marker to write *Happy Birthday* in capital letters around the outside edge of the bowl.

70

step two | Using the white paint marker, on either side of the writing draw a teardrop-shaped mouse with an S-shaped squiggly tail. Then, with a blue fine-tipped paint marker, outline the lettering and add eyes and whiskers to both mice. Outline the mouse ears and dot a nose with a tan fine-tipped paint marker.

Bow Wow Birthday Bowl

Select a larger-size dish and use a red broad-tipped paint marker to write *Happy Bow Wow Day*, separating *Bow* and *Wow* by a large space. With a tan fine-tipped paint marker, outline the letters, and then draw three bones, one before *Happy*, one after *Day* and one in the large space between *Bow* and *Wow*. Outline all three bones with a brown broad-tipped paint marker. Line the finished bowl with colored cellophane and fill it with dog treats. Bring the sides of the cellophane up and tie them together with a ribbon at the top of the dish.

Pet Party Hats

What's a birthday party without hats? These easy-to-make craft foam hats are more durable than their paper counterparts. When they're passed out to pet party guests, it'll be hard to control your laughter and take advantage of the perfect photo opportunity.

materials list

red craft foam

18" (46cm) of ⅛" (3mm) wide elastic

glittered or brightly colored pom-pom

six tiny buttons

¼" (6mm) wide braided elastic trim

scissors

stapler

glue gun

pattern (page 89)

step one | Choose the pattern that fits your pet and cut it out of craft foam. Roll the foam piece into a cone, overlapping the sides by ½" (1cm). Staple the foam layers together at the base. Hot glue the top edge to the bottom edge to finish connecting the sides of the cone.

step two | Fold the 18" (46cm) of elastic in half and knot the ends. Staple the knotted end and the folded end to the sides of the hat.

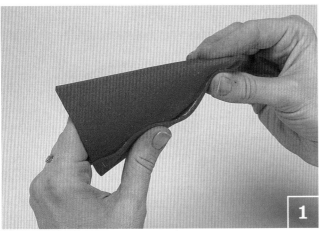

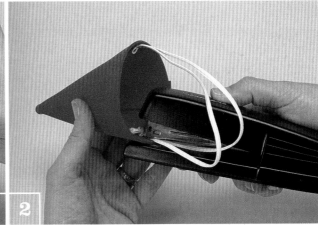

step three | Hot glue the pom-pom to the top of the hat. Hot glue the tiny buttons down the center of the hat and the braided trim around the bottom of the hat.

More Party Hats
These hats are perfect for cats and dogs. Use either the small or large hat pattern on page 89 and decorate the bottom of the hat with multi-colored fringe or chenille rickrack and the sides with star buttons or small pom-poms. Top the hat with a large pom-pom.

Hat:

red craft foam

22" (56cm) of $\frac{1}{8}$" (3mm) wide black elastic

40" (102cm) black shoelace

18" (46cm) piece of gold bootlace

scissors

stapler

glue gun

$\frac{1}{8}$" (3mm) hole punch

patterns (page 90)

Bandanna:

bandanna

1 yard (1m) suede fringe trim

straight pins

sewing machine and white thread

Canine Cowboy Costume

Who can resist Deputy Dawg? Whether your canine thrives on cattle rustling or criminal catching, let his true nature shine through in this easy-to-make Halloween costume. Craft foam is easy to cut, staple and hot glue. You'll be amazed how quickly the pattern pieces will assemble into this crowd-pleasing costume.

step one | Cut the three pattern pieces out of craft foam. Bring the ends of the band piece together, overlap them by ½" (1cm) and staple through the overlapped layers at the top and bottom. Fold the elastic in half and knot the ends together. Staple the knotted end and the folded end to either side of the band piece. Insert the band (elastic end down) ½" (1cm) into the opening in the brim. Center the stapled overlap at the wide end of the opening. Using a small amount of hot glue, anchor the front, back and sides of the band to the brim.

step two | Punch holes around the brim ½" (1cm) apart and ½" (1cm) from the edge. Lace a black shoelace through the holes, starting at the back of the hat. Continue lacing around the hat and then knot the lace ends together under the back edge of the brim.

step three | Hot glue the top of the hat to the top of the band and trim away any overhanging craft foam. Wrap a gold bootlace around the hat and knot it in either the front or back of the hat.

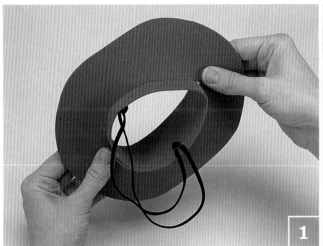

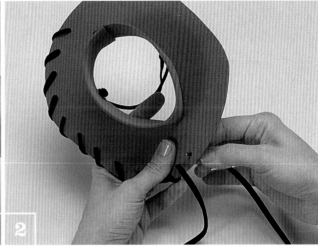

1 2
3 4

step four | Fold the bandanna on the diagonal to make a triangle. Pin the trim to both layers of the bandanna around the two sides. Beginning and ending 1½" (4cm) from the folded ends, sew the fringe to the bandanna. The opening will allow you to thread your dog's collar into the bandanna. This will stop it from sliding off an active dog.

Crafty Cat Witch Costume

Witch feline is the fairest of them all? In this hat, yours, of course. Don't leave all the dress-up fun to the dogs. Some tolerant kitties will deign to don this hat for All Hallows' Eve. Only minutes to make, this hat is a simple variation of the Pet Party Hats (see page 72).

materials list

Hat:

black and gray craft foam

18" (46cm) of ⅛" (3mm) wide black elastic

10" (25cm) of 1" (3cm) wide ribbon

scissors

stapler

glue gun

patterns (page 91)

Bandanna:

bandanna

1" (3cm) thick fusible web

1 yard (1m) suede fringe trim

fabric glue (I used Fabri-Tac)

iron

step one | Cut the small hat pattern from black craft foam. Roll the foam into a cone, overlapping the sides by ½" (1cm). Staple the foam layers together at the base. Hot glue the top edge to the bottom edge to finish connecting the sides of the cone. Fold the 18" (46cm) length of elastic in half and knot the ends. Staple the knotted and folded ends to the sides of the hat. Cut the brim pattern out of black craft foam. Insert the cone, point side down, into the brim opening. Pull the brim down and anchor its connection to the cone with a drop of hot glue at front, back and sides.

step two | Wrap the ribbon around the cone. Hot glue the overlapping ends in the center front of the hat. Cut the buckle pattern pieces out of gray and black craft foam. Hot glue the buckle pieces over the ribbon ends, gluing the solid gray piece first, then the open black piece on top of the gray, and lastly, the small black piece into the center of the open black piece.

step three | Cut the bandanna in half along the diagonal so you are left with two triangles. Set the second triangle aside. Fold the cut edge over 1" (3cm) and then follow the directions on the fusible web to iron the cut edge to the bandanna. Use fabric glue to glue the suede fringe trim around the two finished sides. Tie the finished shawl around your cat's neck.

Pet Christmas Ornaments

materials list

ArtEmboss medium-weight metal sheet

ornament hanger or cord

pencil

scissors

stiffened felt sheet or newspaper

wooden stylus tool

$\frac{1}{8}$" (3mm) hole punch

pattern (page 92)

Pick Your Pattern

PAGE 92 HAS MANY DOG AND CAT PATTERNS TO CHOOSE FROM. PICK THE ONE THAT MOST LOOKS LIKE YOUR PET.

Deck the tree with dogs and cats, fa la la la la, la la. . . . These timeless ornaments will be a yearly reminder of pets present and past. Easy-to-cut metal sheets and screens are widely available and make creating these ornaments a snap. Cut and emboss additional ornaments to match the breeds of friends' and relatives' pets, a thoughtful gift from one pet lover to another.

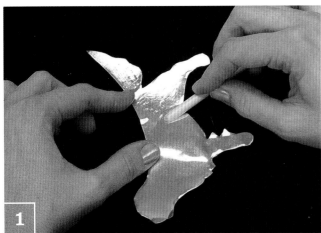

Mesh Ornaments

AMACO, the maker of ArtEmboss, also makes WireMesh, a line of fine-mesh screen sheets. Trace the same patterns onto the screen, then cut and punch as for the metal sheets. The screen can't be shaped to the same degree as the metal, but you can apply slight pressure with a modeling tool to encourage small legs and tails to lie flat. It is easier to cut than the metal, which may tear around tight corners.

step one | Trace the pattern onto the metal sheet and cut out. Lay the shape on the felt (or newspaper) and rub with a wooden stylus tool to rub out the ears and coat texture.

step two | Punch a hole in the top and add an orna-ment hanger.

Pet Christmas Stockings

The puppies and kittens were nestled all snug in their beds while visions of dog bones and mice danced in their heads. This is the perfect holiday craft project for young children. Their first attempts at sewing will be rewarded when they pull out treats for their furry friends on Christmas morning.

materials list

tan, dark brown, red and white craft foam sheets

5' (152cm) plastic craft lacing

9" (23cm) plastic craft lacing (for the stocking hanger)

CraftFoam Glue

scissors

clothespins

⅛" (3mm) hole punch

patterns (page 93)

No Bones About It

INSTEAD OF BONES, USE THE PATTERN ON PAGE 93 AND DECORATE THE STOCKING WITH TENNIS BALLS. SUBSTITUTE THE BONE FOR THE PAW PRINT ON THE STOCKING TOP FOR A NEW LOOK.

step one | Cut two stocking shapes from the tan craft foam. Fasten the layers together with clothespins to prevent them from slipping when punching holes. Beginning at the top, punch holes ½" (1cm) apart and ½" (1cm) in from the outside edge, down one side, around the toe and back up the other side of the stocking. Leave the top of the stocking unpunched.

step two | Cut a 5' (152cm) length of plastic cord. Knot one end and cut the tip of the other end at an angle to make it easier to thread through the holes. Lace the cord through the holes, gently pulling it around the outer edge. Pull gently because too much force will cause the cord to rip out of the holes. If necessary, untwist the cord so the stitches lie flat against the foam. Continue lacing around the stocking, removing the clothespins as you reach them. Knot the end.

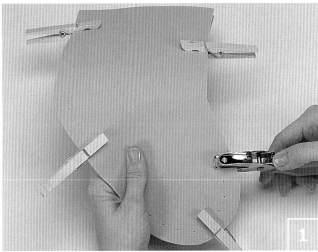
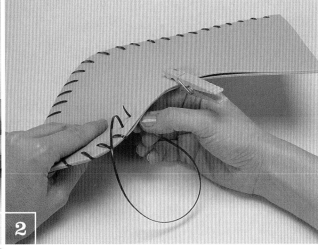

step three | To make a hanger for the stocking, fold a 9" (23cm) length of plastic cord in half and knot the ends. Thread the folded end through the top stocking stitch and pull through; the knot will hold it in place. Next, use the patterns to cut two white stocking tops, one brown and two red bones and a brown paw print. Use CraftFoam Glue to glue all the foam pieces in place. Glue the first stocking top to the back of the stocking, the bones to the front of the stocking, the second stocking top to the front of the stocking (lining it up with the first one), and the paw print to one side of the front stocking top. Let the glue dry completely before use.

Cat Stockings

The cat stockings are cut and stitched the same as for the dog stockings. Cut three mice or fish patterns out of craft foam. Punch out two eyes in each mouse head and one eye in each fish head with a hole punch before gluing them to the stitched stockings. Save the punched dots of craft foam and glue one to the end of each mouse head to make a nose. Cut out the smaller paw pattern and glue it to the stocking cuff.

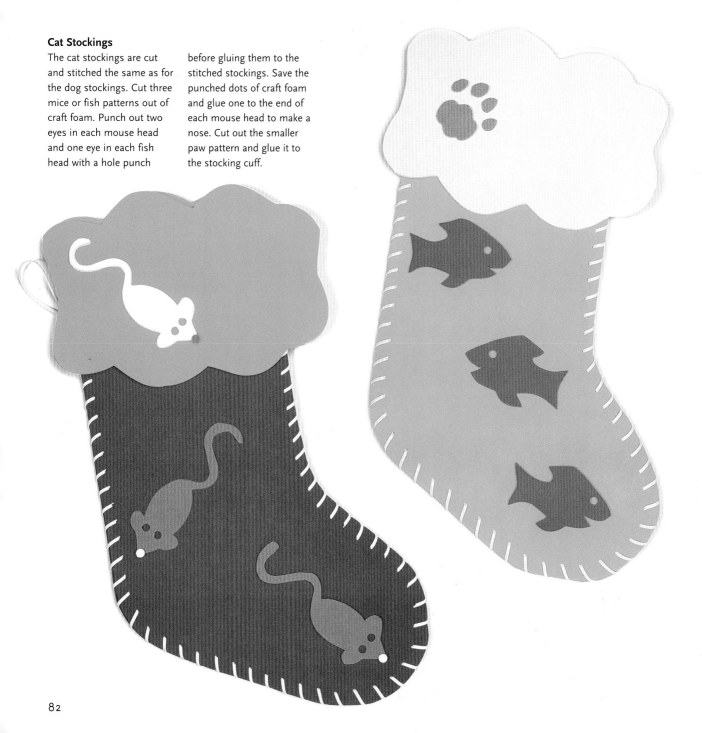

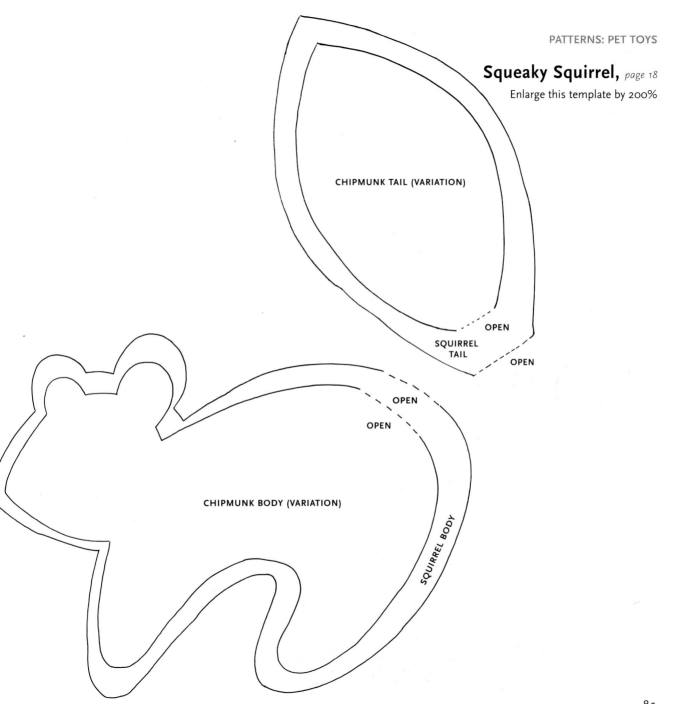

Squeaky Squirrel, *page 18*

Enlarge this template by 200%

CHIPMUNK TAIL (VARIATION)

OPEN

SQUIRREL
TAIL

OPEN

OPEN

OPEN

CHIPMUNK BODY (VARIATION)

SQUIRREL BODY

Puffy Pet Pillows, *page 34*

Enlarge this template by 200%.

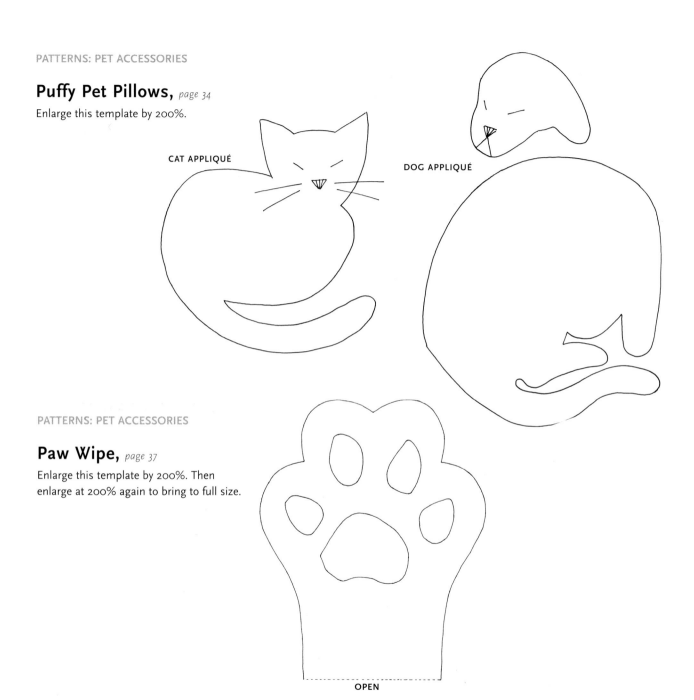

CAT APPLIQUÉ

DOG APPLIQUÉ

Paw Wipe, *page 37*

Enlarge this template by 200%. Then
enlarge at 200% again to bring to full size.

OPEN

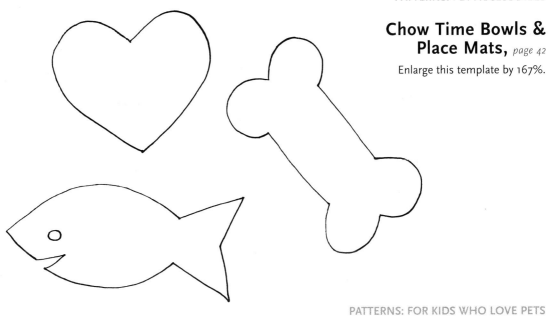

Chow Time Bowls & Place Mats, *page 42*

Enlarge this template by 167%.

Sassy Cat Costume, *page 48*

Enlarge this template by 167%.

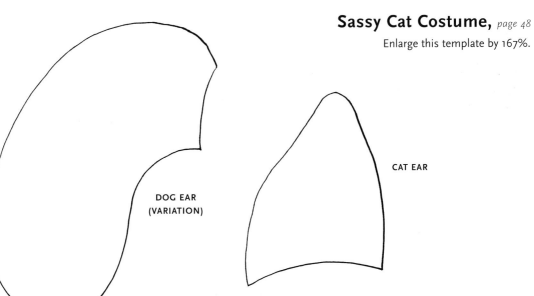

CAT EAR

DOG EAR
(VARIATION)

Fleece Friends, *page 54*

Enlarge this template by 200%. Enlarge
again by 143%.

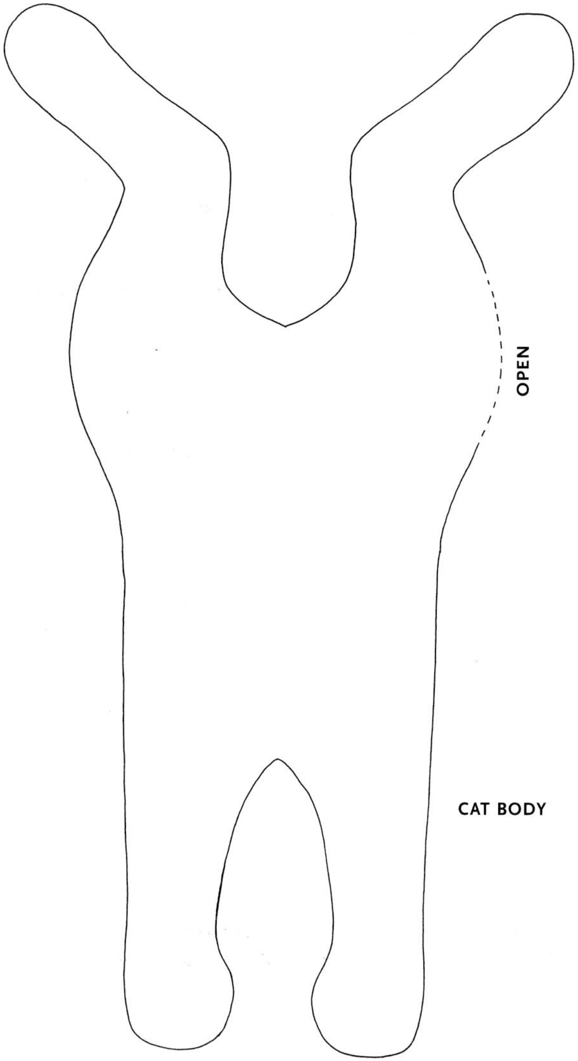

OPEN

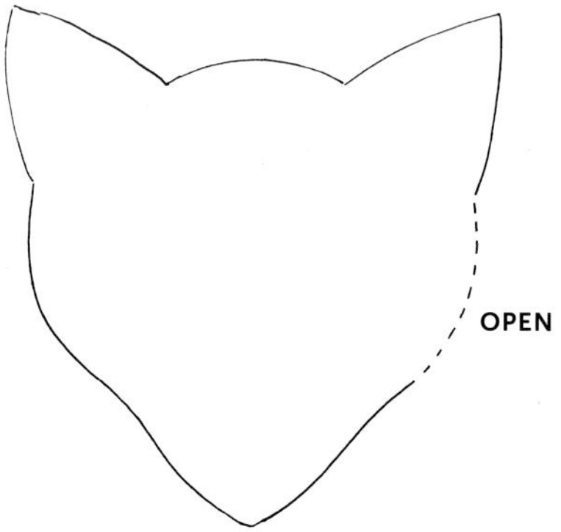

CAT HEAD

CAT TAIL

OPEN

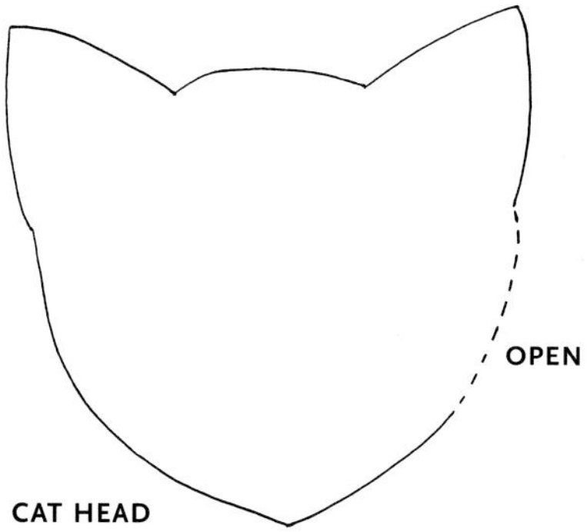

OPEN

CAT HEAD
(VARIATION)

OPEN

CAT NOSE

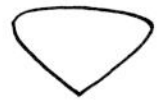

CAT BODY

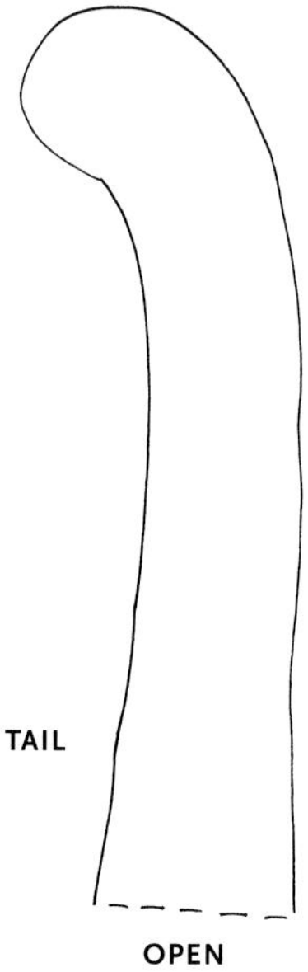

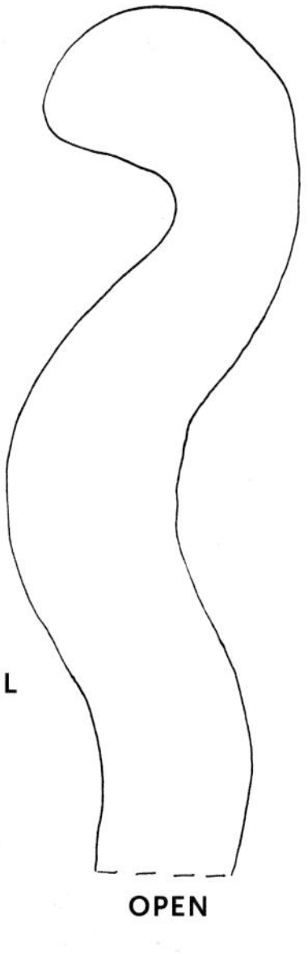

CURLY CAT TAIL
(VARIATION)

OPEN

Fleece Friends, *page 57*

Enlarge this template by 200%. Enlarge
again by 143%.

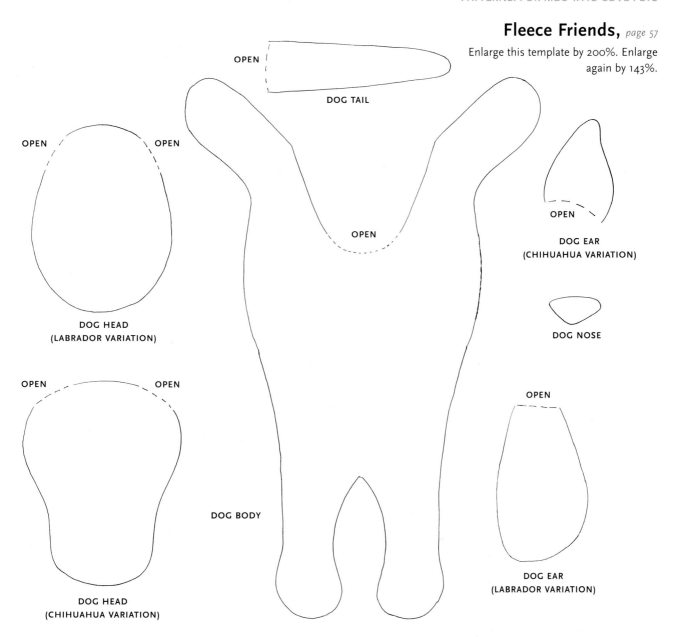

OPEN

DOG TAIL

OPEN   OPEN

DOG HEAD
(LABRADOR VARIATION)

OPEN

DOG EAR
(CHIHUAHUA VARIATION)

OPEN

DOG NOSE

OPEN   OPEN

DOG BODY

DOG HEAD
(CHIHUAHUA VARIATION)

OPEN

DOG EAR
(LABRADOR VARIATION)

Pet Pal Journals, *page 58*

Enlarge this template by 200%.

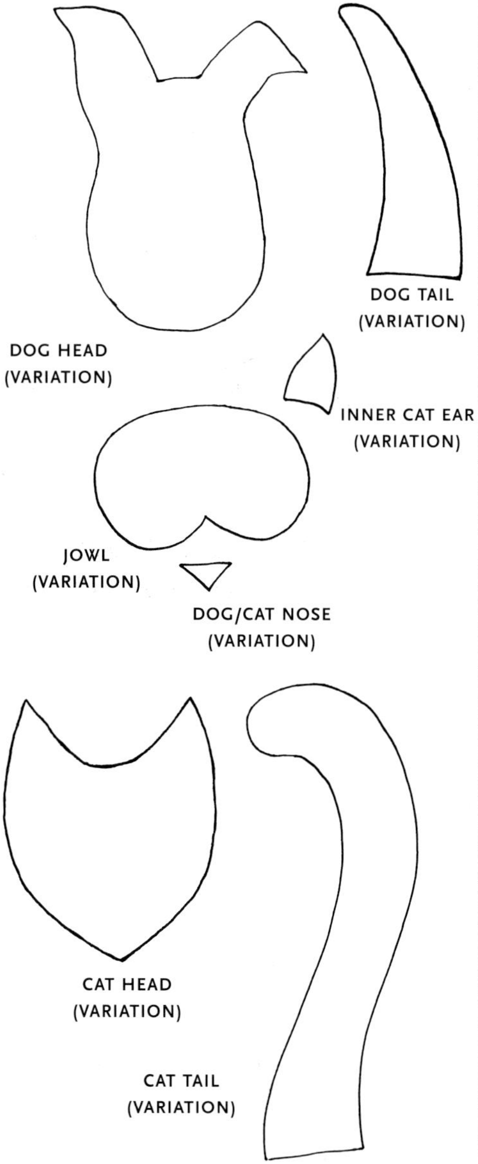

DOG HEAD
(VARIATION)

DOG TAIL
(VARIATION)

INNER CAT EAR
(VARIATION)

JOWL
(VARIATION)

DOG/CAT NOSE
(VARIATION)

CAT HEAD
(VARIATION)

CAT TAIL
(VARIATION)

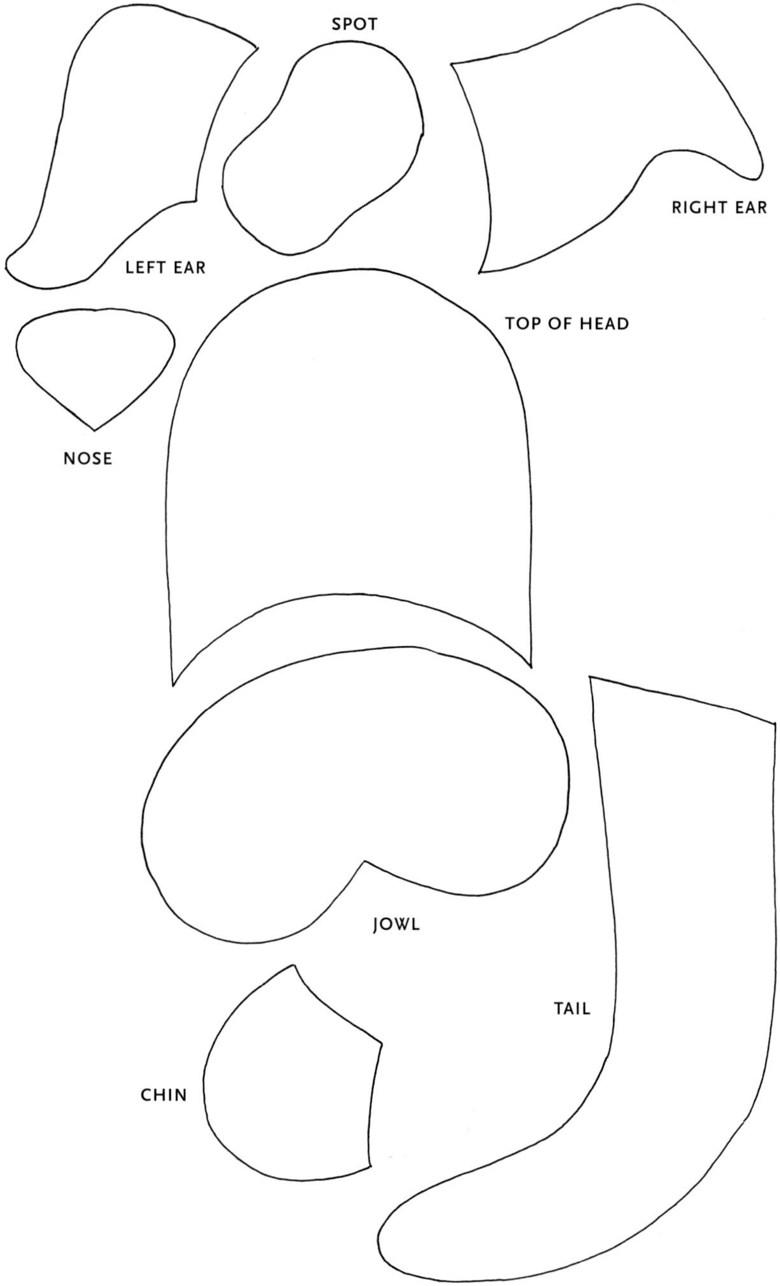

SPOT

LEFT EAR

RIGHT EAR

NOSE

TOP OF HEAD

JOWL

CHIN

TAIL

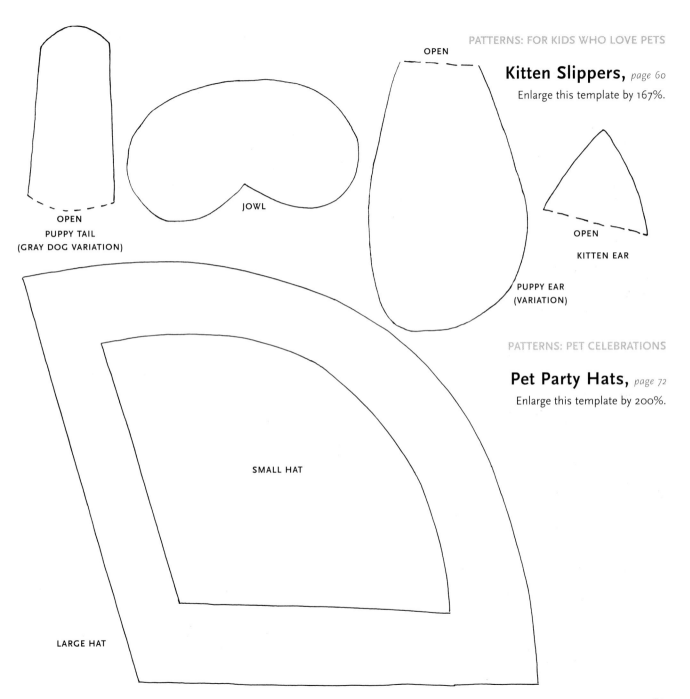

OPEN

Kitten Slippers, *page 60*

Enlarge this template by 167%.

JOWL

OPEN

PUPPY TAIL
(GRAY DOG VARIATION)

OPEN

KITTEN EAR

PUPPY EAR
(VARIATION)

Pet Party Hats, *page 72*

Enlarge this template by 200%.

SMALL HAT

LARGE HAT

Canine Cowboy Costume,

page 74

Enlarge this template by 200%. Enlarge
again by 200%.

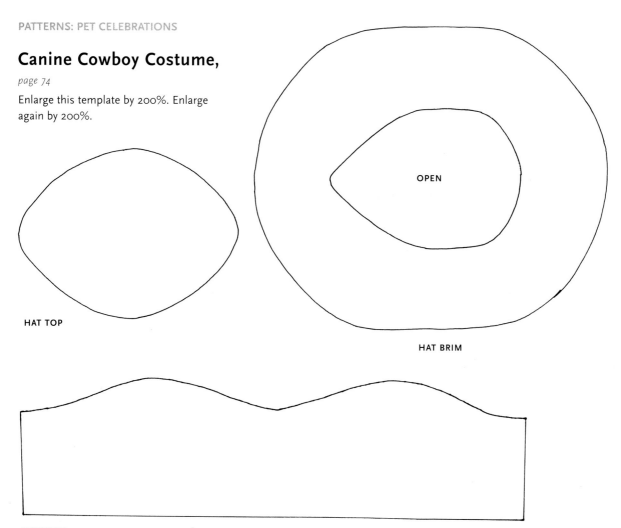

HAT TOP

OPEN

HAT BRIM

HAT BAND

Crafty Cat Witch Costume,

page 76

Enlarge this template by 200%.

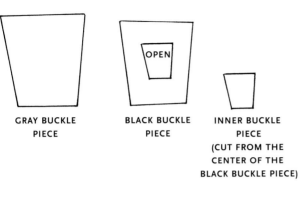

GRAY BUCKLE
PIECE

BLACK BUCKLE
PIECE

INNER BUCKLE
PIECE
(CUT FROM THE
CENTER OF THE
BLACK BUCKLE PIECE)

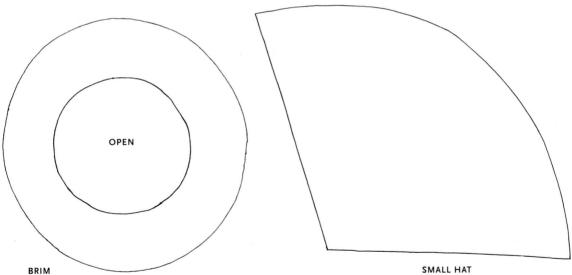

OPEN

BRIM

SMALL HAT

Pet Christmas Ornaments,

page 78

Enlarge this template by 200%.

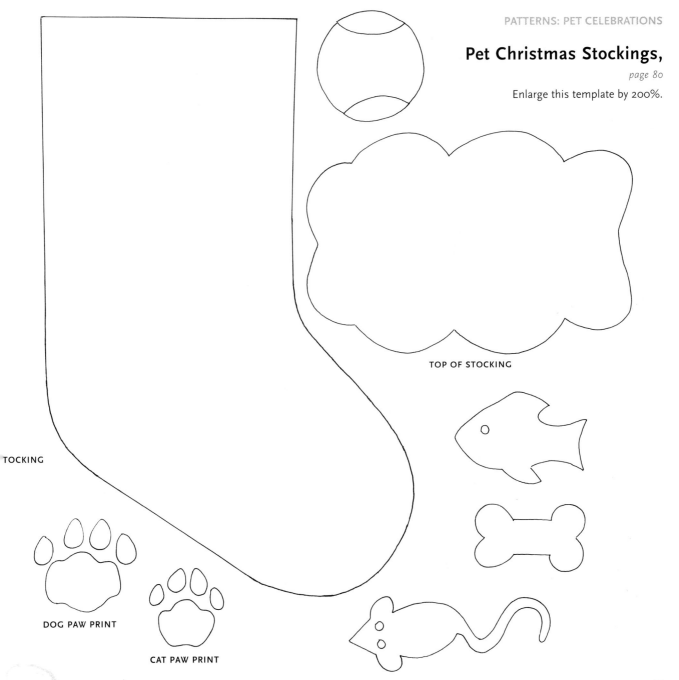

Pet Christmas Stockings,

page 80

Enlarge this template by 200%.

TOP OF STOCKING

TOCKING

DOG PAW PRINT

CAT PAW PRINT

Resource Guide

Most of the materials used in the projects in this book are readily available at discount, pet, fabric and craft stores. For some of the specialized items or specific products used by the author, please see the following guide.

AMACO, AMERICAN ART CLAY CO., INC.
4717 West 16th Street
Indianapolis, IN 46222
(800) 374-1600
www.amaco.com
ArtEmboss medium-weight metal sheets and WireMesh fine-mesh metal screens

DUNCAN ENTERPRISES
5673 East Shields Avenue
Fresno, CA 93727
(800) 438-6226
www.duncancrafts.com
Aleene's Clear Gel Tacky Glue, Aleene's Platinum Bond Glass & Bead Slick Surfaces Adhesive, Aleene's Shrink-It

HERO ARTS
1343 Powell Street
Emeryville, CA 94608
(800) 822-HERO
www.heroarts.com
dog and cat stamps

KUNIN FELT, FOSS MANUFACTURING COMPANY, INC.
380 Lafayette Road
P.o. Box 5000
Hampton, NH 03843-5000
(603) 929-6100
www.kuninfelt.com
Presto Felt

MAKING MEMORIES
1168 West 500 North
Centerville, UT 84014
(801) 294-0430
www.makingmemories.com
eyelet setter, small hammer, metal eyelet charms

MARVY UCHIDA
3535 Del Amo Boulevard
Torrance, CA 90503
(800) 541-5877
www.uchida.com
DecoColor paint markers

PÉBÉO OF AMERICA
www.pebeo.com
Pébéo Porcelaine 150 ceramic pens

PLAID ENTERPRISES, INC.
(800) 842-4197
www.plaidonline.com
All Night Media Classic Alphabet stamp set

RUBBER STAMPEDE
2550 Pellissier Place
Whittier, CA 90601
(800) 423-4135
www.rubberstampede.com
small dog stamps

SIGNATURE CRAFTS
P.O. Box 427
Wycoff, NJ 07481
(800) 865-7238
www.beaconcreates.com
Beacon's CraftFoam Glue, Fabri-Tac, Gem-Tac and Kids Choice Glue

Index

Get creative in your crafts with North Light Books!

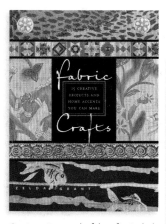

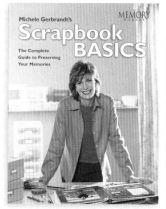

Create unique, colorful crafts, including greeting cards, journal covers, picture frames, wall hangings and more with a world of exciting fabrics. All you need to get started are some old clothes, buttons, coins, cording, faux jewelry and other embellishments. Simple decorative techniques, such as fabric stamping, collage and basic stitching, are clearly explained inside, requiring no prior knowledge of sewing or quilting.
ISBN 1-58180-153-X, paperback, 128 pages, #31902-K

You'll find everything you need to create your own charming birdhouse! Inside are 13 projects complete with step-by-step instructions and color photos using environmentally friendly materials that are readily available. Each birdhouse design creates both a functional and effective habitat for their outdoor companions, and can be used to decorate a spot both indoors and outside.
ISBN 1-58180-071-1, paperback, 128 pages, #31793-K

Packed with helpful instruction and illustrations, this book provides all the information you need to create your own scrapbooks with confidence! Michele shows you how to select the most useful starter supplies, organize photos and negatives and set up an efficient workspace. You'll also find tips on designing page layouts, cropping photos, adding journal entries, and brainstorming ideas.
ISBN 1-89212-716-4, paperback, 128 pages, #32417-K

These easy-to-follow techniques enable you to accurately render a variety of wonderful animals, from cats and dogs to horses, squirrels, tigers and more. Artist Lee Hammond's special graphing system helps your brain translate the animal poses you see into drawings on the page. You'll also learn other important illustration techniques and guidelines to help you duplicate realistic eyes, ears, mouths, feet, fur, and hide.
ISBN 1-58180-273-0, paperback, 80 pages, #32144-K

These books and other fine titles are available from your local art & craft retailer, bookstore, online supplier or by calling 1-800-448-0915.